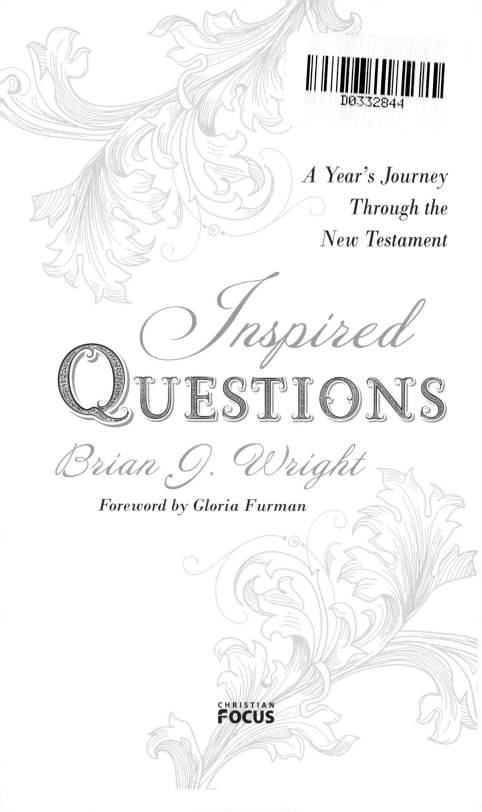

A Year's Journey
Through the
New Testament

Inspired
QUESTIONS

Brian J. Wright

Foreword by Gloria Furman

CHRISTIAN
FOCUS

Copyright © Brian J. Wright 2019

paperback ISBN 978-1-5271-0423-5
epub ISBN 978-1-5271-0492-1
mobi ISBN 978-1-5271-0493-8

10 9 8 7 6 5 4 3 2 1

Published in 2019
by
Christian Focus Publications Ltd,
Geanies House, Fearn, Ross-shire,
IV20 1TW, Great Britain.

www.christianfocus.com

Cover and interior design by Rubner Durais

Printed and bound
by Bell & Bain, Glasgow

Inspired Questions is very accessible and needed, and I am glad to see it in print. Read it with an open bible, an open heart, and an open door for others to join you!

J. P. MORELAND
Distinguished Professor of Philosophy, Talbot School of Theology,
Biola University, La Mirada, California
author of *Finding Quiet*

I love how Brian Wright has designed a devotional led by the questions in Scripture. Questions are confrontational. And these inspired questions get to the heart of the matter. Reflecting on one of these questions each day, and then reading Brian's take-action commentary will be time well spent.

AIMEE BYRD
author of *No Little Women* and *Why Can't We Be Friends?*

As soon as I saw Brian's book, I thought, 'Eureka! Why has no one done this before?' What a marvellous idea to deal with the questions that the Bible deems worthy to deal with. God knows the snags in our thinking and addresses them before we do. This book will be a blessing to all who read it!

TOMMY NELSON
Senior Pastor, Denton Bible Church, Denton, Texas
author of several best-selling books including *The Book of Romance*, *A Life Well Lived* and *Walking on Water When You Feel Like You're Drowning*

Devotional books are often a source of hackneyed shibboleths or spiritual sentimentalism. Not so with Brian Wright's *Inspired Questions: A Year's Journey through the New Testament!* With 365 pointed questions from the New Testament, Wright daily confronts his readers with spiritual truth. Accompanying each Scriptural question are brief devotional reflections that are hermeneutically-informed and relevant to modern-day readers. I'll be taking this book home and reading the daily devotions around the family breakfast table this coming week.

ROBERT L. PLUMMER
Founder, Daily Dose of Greek
Professor, New Testament Interpretation,
The Southern Baptist Theological Seminary, Louisville, Kentucky

Brian Wright has written a biblically saturated, yet wonderfully practical devotional for the twenty-first-century church. Indeed, it is written in such a simple (yet profound) way that I would feel comfortable giving it out to any church member. Each question is expounded biblically, understood communally, and leads to numerous implications and applications. For the reader who is in the habit of journaling, be prepared to have a second pen on hand, as your ink will run dry by mid-year. I highly recommend that you read this insightful devotional, and then read it again with others!

JAMES J. ACKERMAN
President and CEO, Prison Fellowship

The Bible is filled with questions – both from God and mankind. *Inspired Questions* is a devotional that takes a deeper look at some of those questions, challenging readers to evaluate their hearts. This unique devotional will have readers asking questions of their own hearts as they seek to grow and apply God's word to their lives.

CHRISTINA FOX
writer, speaker, author of *Idols of a Mother's Heart* and
Sufficient Hope: Gospel Meditations and Prayers for Moms.

Every once in a great while a book comes along that is so compelling in its force and so obvious in its approach that one wonders why no one had thought of it before. This is one of those books. Brian Wright is a biblical scholar with a gift for effortless clarity and penetrating simplicity. In brief, he reiterates the questions in the Bible and guides us on a path of reflection, repentance, and reverence. Devour these *Inspired Questions* and see your life transformed!

DANIEL B. WALLACE
Senior Research Professor of New Testament Studies,
Dallas Theological Seminary, Dallas, Texas

If you are looking for a fresh approach to engage Scripture, this is the devotional for you. Brian uses questions asked by Jesus, the disciples and others for each devotional and challenges the reader to interact with Scripture through reflection and application.

KAREN SWANSON
Director of the Institute for Prison Ministries, Billy Graham Center,
Wheaton College, Wheaton, Illinois

CONTENTS

For Neriah, Zephaniah, Jedidiah, and Hezekiah –

'I have no greater joy
than to hear that my children are walking in the truth.'
3 John 4

Foreword

Most days tumble together and pass into the past at breakneck speed. Can you remember the content of the conversation you had with a friend last week? How easy is it to recall the headlines of yesterday's news? Do you know what time you ate breakfast today? 'Carpe diem!' they say. But, alas. The days slip from our grasp so quickly.

In this age of push notifications that compel our attention to the next thing and the next thing, I'd love to slow my pace. Enjoy the respite of a breeze on a humid day. Enjoy the intensity of watching my kids' swim meet. Enjoy the wonder of waking up to a new day. Enjoy the waterfall of future grace that is tumbling into my life every moment, because of the person and work of Jesus Christ.

I suspect that you'd like to slow down and enjoy life more, too. But where do we go from here? I think questions afford us the reflective pause we need in our fast-paced societies.

When I worked in a university residence hall I kept a jar of 'Intentional Questions' on my desk. Residents would come in for a meeting and I'd invite them to choose a question from the jar for discussion. 'What's something you wish more people knew about you?' 'Why do you think it is so hard for people to ask for help?' Those questions sparked thoughtful conversations and gave me windows of insight into my residents' lives.

How much more do the questions in God's inspired Word offer us a chance to pause, reflect, and marvel at the character and work of our Creator!

Sit still with the questions in this book. Or better yet, stand, and walk, and run, and lie down with these questions on your mind. Allow

them to scrutinize your heart motives. Discuss them with your kids and your friends. See how the Spirit highlights the aching desire of your heart and it's incredible fulfillment: knowing and being known by God. Learn to ask (and keep asking!) this question with Asaph and revel in its glorious answer, 'Whom have I in heaven but you? And there is nothing on earth that I desire besides you' (Ps. 73:25).

GLORIA FURMAN
Pastor's wife, Mom of four

Blogger and Author of several books including
Missional Motherhood and *Alive in Him*

Introduction

The Decades Leading up to This Devotional

In 1999, as a junior in college, I was hit with numerous thought-provoking questions I had never heard or considered before as a non-Christian. On many occasions I wished I had been asked them earlier in my life instead of enduring the bad decisions, broken relationships, and pain I had already experienced.

Those penetrating, life-changing questions were not the result of someone's witty concoctions—no, not one. All of the questions that pierced my soul and spirit that year came directly from God's Word after one of my teammates challenged me to read the Bible for the first time. I realized that while I didn't yet have answers, I could find them through studying Scriptural truth and finding a personal application to them.

After college, I spent the next eleven years climbing the ranks of corporate America within several Fortune 100 companies. I started as an intern for one corporation. I finished as an executive for another. Life was relatively easy during those final years: six-figure salary, high-rise office in a major city, and travels around the world.

Then in August of 2010, after completing a Master in Theology (Th.M.) degree at Dallas Theological Seminary, I left the corporate world for good to become a full-time pastor. Shortly after leaving my job, God opened up a door for me to pastor within the Federal Bureau of Prisons. Like most people, I had never been behind prison walls before. Yet I had no doubt God was calling me to this unconventional ministry.

From 2011 to now, I have served in every federal security level (camp, low, medium, high, administrative), custody level (in, out, max, community), and gender grouping available in the Federal Bureau of Prisons. I have had the privilege of counseling, pastoring, and assisting countless inmates, including bank presidents, entertainers, professional athletes, international terrorists, murderers, sex offenders, drug lords, prostitutes, illegal immigrants, and other convicts. Listening to their stories firsthand and walking alongside them in the aftermath of their federal crimes has helped me see the timeless truths of the Scriptures played out in real life, as well as appreciate the Christ-centered hope available in every situation.

In 2012, one year after walking into a prison for the first time, God gave me the idea for this series of short readings based on questions in the Bible. The idea immediately led to prayer. Prayer led to preparation. Preparation included a Ph.D. in New Testament Studies and Early Christian Origins. It was in this context, ministering in prison full time and obtaining my doctorate, that I wrote a draft of the book you are reading.

I finished the first draft of it in May 2017. Then I put it away for exactly one year before looking at it again and going back through it. I'm sure glad I did. Little did I know, God had much more in store for it than I had initially thought.

Why I Wrote This Devotional

I wrote this collection of short, easy-to-read devotions under the conviction that you cannot get to the right answers until you have the right questions—and that the greatest questions ever asked are inspired ones. The Bible alone stands as the source and storehouse of inspired questions. It asks questions we could never ask ourselves. Yet, no one has ever written a 365-day devotional based entirely on the questions already asked in the New Testament.

I also wrote it because a substantial portion of our Bible is questions, and asking questions was a primary teaching method of Jesus. To put this in perspective, the Book of Proverbs has approximately 930 sayings, while the New Testament alone contains about 980 questions.

Of course, we find inspired questions throughout the whole Bible, not just in the New Testament. Satan first approached Eve with a question in the Garden of Eden (Gen. 3:1). When the angel of the Lord first

appears in the Bible, he asks a question (Gen. 16:8). When the Witch of Endor conjures up Samuel from the dead, he immediately asks Saul questions (1 Sam. 28:15-16). When God finally speaks to Job, He addresses him with questions (Job 38–41). When the angel Gabriel first appears in the Book of Daniel, he starts with a question (Dan. 8:13). It's somewhat of a paradox that the importance of Scriptural questions is unquestionable.

Finally, I wrote this work out of a need I identified through both personal experience and pastoral counseling. I can personally testify that meditating on these inspired questions has radically changed my life and ministry. My marriage has been positively impacted because of them, such as the ones posed in James 4:1. I have been able to handle more effectively several major issues in my church after wrestling with the question in Galatians 4:16. My counseling benefited from questions such as the one found in Luke 12:25. Indeed, there are many others: witnessing and missions via Romans 10:14; communion via 1 Corinthians 10:16; and parenting via Hebrews 12:7; just a few among more than 900 still to explore.

Inspired Questions: A Year's Journey through the New Testament

Pause for a moment and imagine this: People in the first century heard every question you are about to read. Many of the questions are ones Jesus Himself heard or asked. It is now time for you—the twenty-first century listener—to hear the same questions.

Just as a doctor asks many questions in order to determine whether you are at low, medium, or high risk for whatever ails you, this devotional contains 365 X-ray-like questions for your soul and spirit. They will help you determine your spiritual state. They will urge you to change your focus, reorder your affections, and reprioritize your loves. They will compel you to love God more fervently and selflessly, while weaning your heart off the lies and lures of this world. They will enable you to cope with adversity, tear down strongholds, and achieve what would otherwise be impossible—the mastery over your experiences through the intellectual, emotional, and spiritual state of biblical wisdom. They will also inspire you to action, not just sweet reflections. You

will quickly realize that these inspired questions reveal your heart in ways other methods do not.

You should put these inspired questions into your mental medicine cabinet, especially for when you are going through tough times. The questions are never just about finding answers. They are always about advancing your understanding and strengthening your walk with the Lord and others. They are designed to compel you to do something more than just read.

Instead of just providing you with quick take-it-or-leave-it answers, the questions compel you to think through the implications yourself. They coax you to slow down. We all too often forget how easily we can derail from the right path of life.

Ways to Get the Most from this Devotional

Most of you will probably find that reading one entry a day as part of your time alone with God will work best. For others, perhaps you will use this book communally, as you discuss these questions as part of your family worship, readings with your kids, or Bible studies with your church community. Still others of you may go through this book with someone you are discipling or with a person who is wrestling with the Christian faith in order to discuss these poignant questions with them—recalling that Jesus used many of these questions to engage His disciples and culture.

Whatever you (all) decide, after you read each entry, reflect on it. Sit there and ponder until it addresses you personally. Seek God, not the answer. If you seek God, you will discover the truth as it applies to you.

After you read and reflect, respond. Determine your response. Be honest. Face the questions. Face them with absolute honesty. Each inspired question is for you, not just the church and others. God deserves your best, and others are counting on you.

Perhaps you might wish to journal as well. Consider one or more of these interactive ways to engage each entry:

- Paraphrase your understanding of the question(s) and short reflection.

- Write one or two sentences on how you plan on applying it to your life.

- Describe how someone you admire has applied the truth you gleaned.

- Note what it means for your community and the Body of Christ.

- Draw a picture of how it impacts you.

- Write two lines of poetry based on the question.

- Jot down what fruit of the Spirit is being displayed.

- List an attribute of God that comes to mind and what that attribute means to you.

- Summarize how it connects to your life and awakens you to the needs of others.

In the midst of all this, pray. Pray before, during, and some more after each day's devotion. Spiritual growth is a spiritual matter. So pray that God makes this journey rich and that each day you will walk away from this time never quite being the same. The fruit of this book will only come by living out the truths gleaned from it.

It is also important to highlight that this collection of questions is merely a supplement to reading them in their inspired context, the Bible. My hope is that each entry drives you deeper into your own reading of the Holy Scriptures. Some readers will immediately know the context of the question(s), but others will not. Additional passages—one from the Old Testament and one from the New Testament—appear at the end of each entry for further study and reflection. The year's journey will generally follow the church calendar, which includes Advent, Christmas, Epiphany, Lent, Holy Week, and Eastertide. But you do not need to understand or follow a liturgical calendar to benefit from this devotional.

I hope this devotional thrills you. I hope it makes you want more out of your Christian life. I pray that you will never be like the people mentioned in Paul's second letter to Timothy: 'always learning and never able to arrive at a knowledge of the truth' (3:7). Rather, I pray this devotional will foster a closer relationship with you and your precious Savior, Jesus Christ, as well as others around you.

Remember, on Judgment Day, our Lord will not ask you what devotionals you have read, but what deeds you have done. With that in mind, take a moment to (re)consider and pray the words of the Psalmist before you begin: 'Search me, O God, and know my heart! Try me and know my thoughts! And see if there be any grievous way in me, and lead me in the way everlasting!' (Ps. 139:23-24).

January

'After three days they found him in the temple, sitting among the teachers, listening to them and asking them questions.'

– Luke 2:46

> *'For if you love those who love you,*
> *what reward do you have?'*
> – Matthew 5:46

You do not have to be a Christian to love, help, or give to people. In fact, you do not even need a religion, faith, or commandment to do it. Everyone instinctively prioritizes those who love them. But Jesus wants to completely transform your thoughts and actions; indeed, your very nature. The person you most despise, disapprove of, or dislike is exactly who He wants you to love. Such supernatural love is only possible when you follow Jesus. No other so-called god encourages this type of love, but your God does! This type of love is exactly what Jesus calls you to shine forth in this world. Jesus also modeled it for you. When struck, He did not strike back. When ridiculed, He did not ridicule in return. When nailed to the cross, He prayed for His enemies.

Of course, this inspired question reveals more about you than just your external behaviors. The way you treat other people exposes the true inclinations of your heart. Apart from Christ, you are utterly selfish. But Christ has given you a new heart.

Therefore, by the power of the Holy Spirit, go beyond this world's expectation and love those who cannot or will not love you in return. This love does not necessarily mean liking someone or pretending sin is not evident. God loves sinners by providing rain and sunlight on the righteous and unrighteous alike. You can love them as He does by treating them equally, providing for them, and being a source of blessing.

2 Kings 6:20-23; John 15:12-17

For what does the Scripture say?

– Romans 4:3

When you discuss things, this inspired question ought to be on the tip of your tongue. It should be your most asked question, even if just in your mind. What does God think and say, not just people? The inspired and infallible Word of God must illuminate every question you have; every truth you accept.

Be an excellent student of God's Word. Bring up others in the instruction of the Lord. Continually appeal to the Scriptures. Store God's Word in your heart.

Deuteronomy 11:18; 2 Timothy 3:16

'Who is worthy to open the scroll and break its seals?'

– Revelation 5:2

Imagine finding something of infinite value—but you cannot open it because it is sealed or locked. How disheartening! The good news for you, however, is that Christ is able to unlock everything. He unlocks the true meaning of the Old Testament. He unlocks the door of salvation. He unlocks an eternal inheritance. Christ alone has authority over judgment and redemption because He is worthy. Still more, Christ is worthy to open the scroll and break its seals because He suffered the wrath of God for you as your sinless substitute, paying the penalty for your sins.

No matter what you suffer in this life, you can find comfort in the answer to this inspired question. Christ is worthy enough to open God's Word and accomplish His purposes, and you are firmly established in Him as a believer. Your eternal destiny is secure. Continue abiding in Christ.

Isaiah 29:11-12; Hebrews 3:3

'Sirs, what must I do to be saved?'
– Acts 16:30

What a simple—yet profound—question. You want deliverance. And what a simple—yet profound—answer: 'Believe in the Lord Jesus.' You can be delivered by believing in Jesus Christ. Such belief involves confession, trust, and commitment, not merely intellectual understanding. You may have sought for help, answers, and happiness elsewhere. But they will not be found in this world. The deepest longings of your heart will only be satisfied when you are in a right relationship with God the Father through God the Son by means of God the Holy Spirit.

Commit your life to Him. Do not keep delaying!

Proverbs 28:13; John 3:1-15

Who has bewitched you?
– Galatians 3:1

Are you bewitched? Has someone put you under their spell? According to the Apostle Paul, it doesn't take a witch to bewitch you. When you fall under any evil influence, you can be lured away from God into false doctrine, worldliness, or sin. Jesus calls His followers sheep, for we are all weak and prone to wander.

Therefore, you must stay very close to your Shepherd. Listen to His voice in His Word and call for Him when you stray. Remain with His flock by being active in a local church. Beware of wolves, especially those in sheep's clothing. Follow Jesus closely. Read the Bible daily. Pray regularly. Participate in church faithfully. Evaluate your friends and teachers carefully. Don't be bewitched!

Jeremiah 14:14; Matthew 7:15

'Are you the one who is to come, or shall we look for another?'
– Luke 7:19

You may experience times when your faith, the church, or Jesus falls short of your expectations. You thought the outcome would be different. You expected to see or experience something else. But Jesus' answer to this inspired question means you can trust the Word of God despite your circumstances or the emotions that are stirred up by them. God doesn't always work within your time frame or according to your expectations, but His Word is always true.

Thus, remember this: God may not be early in fulfilling His promises, but He is never late. Accept God's timing. Trust in Him.

Micah 5:2; John 4:25

'Why does this man speak like that?
He is blaspheming!
Who can forgive sins but God alone?'
– Mark 2:7

Only God can forgive sins. Anyone who claims to do what only God can do threatens the unique status of the one true God.

The implications of this eternal truth are still enormously important for you today. Jesus has the authority to forgive and heal sinners because He is God. The deep reality of what He has done for you ought to evoke a deep response of devotion. Invest intentional time today reflecting on this truth. Stand in awe of the one true God, who eternally exists as three persons. Worship Him.

Deuteronomy 6:4; Romans 9:4-5

> *How much worse punishment, do you*
> *think, will be deserved by the one who has*
> *trampled underfoot the Son of God, and*
> *has profaned the blood of the covenant*
> *by which he was sanctified, and has*
> *outraged the Spirit of grace?*
> — Hebrews 10:29

It is difficult to imagine that anyone would reject God's Law when God has done so much for them. Yet think about how much more unbelievable it is when someone today denies Jesus, insults the Holy Spirit, and rejects the New Covenant, which has so many blessings to offer them. The punishment for rejecting the New Covenant is far greater than rejecting the Old Covenant.

This is the highest form of contempt. Jesus is our Mediator; the perfect sacrifice; the radiance of God's glory. He is exalted and enthroned at the right hand of God. To reject Him is to reject God's forgiveness and love. To infuriate the source of your salvation, the Spirit of grace, who was sent by God, is to reject Christ's work. Resolve to be a child of God. Surrender yourself to Him and His ways. Thank God for His mercies.

Leviticus 24:13-16; Matthew 11:20-24

'If you love those who love you, what
benefit is that to you?'
– Luke 6:32

The world operates on reciprocity—nationally and individually. We expect positive results from our kindnesses. Extending love and helping people who are unlikely or unable to return it, on the contrary, is what Jesus demands. It is supernatural.

Be willing to love, do good, and lend to those who will never return your kindness. Expect nothing back. Assume your action is a one-way street, not a two-way street. Your motives should be pure, not self-interested. People who expect something in return are ordinary people, unbelievers. You—as one of God's people—are different. Aspire to noble tasks. Be self-sacrificing. Be like Christ.

Exodus 23:4-5; Matthew 7:12

Do you not know that your bodies are members of Christ?
Shall I then take the members of Christ and make them
members of a prostitute?
– 1 Corinthians 6:15

Your spiritual life cannot be separated from your physical life. In fact, your body is a place for God's presence to be seen. Sexual immorality communicates ignorance of this biblical truth. Being united with Christ through His resurrection and being united with a prostitute through intercourse is unacceptable. Do not combine the two. Your body matters—and it is the Lord's because Christ died for you. You have been joined to Christ. It is unthinkable (not to mention unbiblical) that you would even contemplate being a part of both Christ and anything that defiles your body—sexual immorality; gluttony; drugs; etc.

Consider your body. Discipline your body. Ignore the noises of this world. Listen wholeheartedly to the voice of truth.

Genesis 2:24; Ephesians 5:31-32

> *'Why do you question these*
> *things in your hearts?'*
> – Mark 2:8

Only God is all-knowing, knowing even the thoughts and intentions of your heart. Jesus is able to do what only God can do because He is God, the second person of the Trinity. And knowing your heart, Jesus does not remain quiet and hope for the best. He discerns your inner turmoil and asks you a question—one requiring you to examine your heart and innermost thoughts.

Remembering that He knows you inside and out, think about this inspired question, which becomes all the more powerful and telling. Consider this inspired question prayerfully in God's presence. Ask for discernment. Jesus has all authority and power to heal and forgive. Believe that He is able to do for you exceedingly abundantly above all that you could ask or think.

2 Kings 17:14; 1 John 2:22-23

Who is it that overcomes the world
except the one who believes that
Jesus is the Son of God?

– 1 John 5:5

To overcome opposition in this world, you must continue believing in the only person who has ever conquered the world: Jesus Christ, the Son of God. Holding on to your belief may be difficult at times, especially with the world's propaganda. Society has done well here, blinding the eyes of people.

Jesus is not merely a person, but the Son of God. The power of God was revealed in His Son, and the Son used divine power to overcome the world. This power is greater than the evil one, Satan. You cannot believe anything less about Jesus because otherwise He would not have the power to save you from sin, Satan, and death. Your faith in the Son of God enables you also to overcome the world, for He lives in you. Consider the abundant mercies God has given you. Name any problem you have and there is a wave of divine mercies to wash it away. Labor to have your thoughts on things above.

Psalm 27; John 16:33

Who shall separate us from the love of Christ? Shall
tribulation, or distress, or persecution, or famine, or
nakedness, or danger, or sword?

– Romans 8:35

How little you merit God's love, yet it is yours in Christ. It is perfect and complete, lacking in nothing. His love for you has no end. That is why nothing can separate you from the love of Christ. It is overwhelming. Nothing ought to disturb your faith because you have Christ's love.

Now think about how Christ's love should transform you and illuminate the darkest areas of your life. Consider this realization carefully and pray extensively. Begin implementing it into your life this week.

Deuteronomy 7:9; John 15:9

JANUARY 14

Do you not realize this about yourselves,
that Jesus Christ is in you?—unless
indeed you fail to meet the test!

– 2 Corinthians 13:5

There are good reasons why doctors have you answer questions about yourself—even sometimes with a point system to determine if you are of low, medium, or high risk. In a similar way, you should have a strong, biblically-based, self-awareness assessment. Examine your calling and test the genuineness of your faith. Examine your conduct and theology. Scrutinize your thoughts and attitudes.

Do you have a way of testing yourself? Have you been deceiving yourself? When you look at yourself in a mirror (both physically and metaphorically), do you see someone who is living by means of the Spirit? Call these things into question. Test yourself today. Show prompt obedience. Always look to Jesus.

Lamentations 3:40; James 1:23-25

*Have you not then made distinctions among yourselves
and become judges with evil thoughts?*

– James 2:4

Do not show favoritism, especially based on appearances. Discrimination is contrary to the Christian faith. It stands opposite the model of Jesus. It offends God. It clashes with what is taught in the Scriptures. Unfortunately, though, discrimination can sneak into the church. When it does, it weakens the Christian community. It damages the church's reputation. It provokes God's anger.

Never, then, show favoritism. Never deny God in your actions by showing partiality. If you do, you are putting yourself in the same place as a crooked judge who gives rulings based on a bias or bribe. Such premeditated decision-making (or 'evil thoughts,' in the words of this question) reveals a perverted worldview—not a Christian one. Your approach to life must be different. Pursue the things that make for peace. Believe the best in others. Give people the benefit of the doubt.

Leviticus 19:15; Galatians 5:13-15

*If someone does not know how to manage his own
household, how will he care for God's church?*

– 1 Timothy 3:5

You know the answer: 'He won't.' How you behave in private impacts how well you can lead in public. God expects you to do in your home what you are doing elsewhere: working hard, resolving problems, promoting unity, and displaying love.

If you are successful in your home, you will probably be successful wherever you go. But if you are ineffective with the people you live with, you are inadequate to care for anyone else. As a Christian, it is vital that you live the gospel message at home as well as outside the home. Revive your home, work, and life in light of this truth.

2 Samuel 12:9-15; 1 Timothy 5:8

'Who is like the beast, and who can fight against it?'
— Revelation 13:4

Throughout the Bible, Satan has been imitating truth. He can even disguise himself as an angel of light. Many people align themselves with him because of it. They praise things in this world, instead of God. What results is that you see a question about God's power on the lips of people who have already decided that Satan is greater than God.

Such a question blasphemes God. They magnify themselves above God. They attach themselves to all sorts of false religion. They even challenge anyone to prove the beast wrong, meaning that they do not just speak well of the beast but magnify him as if he is the greatest god.

You have probably seen this light-hearted approach to Satan. Aside from horror films, there are almost no horrific depictions of sin, Satan, or evil forces today. Notice how many menus include them (chocolate decadent cake; sinful sundae), sports teams parade them (New Jersey Devils; Blue Devils), and products brand them (Sinful Clothing Collection; Dirt Devil). There really is no true recognition of how bad sin, Satan, and evil forces really are. Open your eyes. Be on guard. Take up the cross of Jesus. Follow Him.

Daniel 11:31-37; 2 Thessalonians 2:1-12

'Who do people say that the Son of Man is?'
– Matthew 16:13

You are going to be around non-Christians in this world. At various times, you will hear what people say about Jesus and how they categorize Him: teacher, prophet, good man, or something else.

Educate them when possible. Explain how important it is to understand who Jesus is and what He has done for us. Pick out one or two key verses with which to persuade them. Pray earnestly. Remember that to confess Him as Lord will be a divine act through divine revelation. It involves confessing Jesus to be the Messiah, the Son of the living God.

Do not forget to take time also to delight yourself in knowing Him as Lord. *Daniel 7:13-14; John 3:13-15*

'Who are my mother and my brothers?'
– Mark 3:33

The family of Jesus is broader than you may think. He advocates a greater degree of unity when His followers meet than merely an ad hoc get-together. In fact, spiritual relationships supersede biological ones. What is of the flesh is flesh, and what is of the spirit is spirit. Jesus' ultimate family, and thus your ultimate family, consists of those who do God's will: they look to Jesus and believe in Him.

You may even lose your biological family because you are following Jesus. The good news, however, is that you belong to an eternal family. You are established in God's family, the church. Live in light of this promise. Let others see you prioritize God and His family.

Psalm 22:22-24; Hebrews 2:11-13

> *Is Christ divided? Was Paul crucified for you?*
> *Or were you baptized in the name of Paul?*
> — 1 Corinthians 1:13

The expected answer to all three inspired questions here is an emphatic, 'No!' You must decide what you believe and how you will act. There is only one Christ. Only Jesus was crucified for you. You were baptized in the name of the Father and of the Son and of the Holy Spirit—no one else. Do not be misled by divisions, cults of personality, or artificial rivalries we humans have created. We are united in Christ. There ought to be unity, not disunity; harmony, not disharmony; peace, not conflict.

Continually work to preserve the unity of the body of Christ. Pause now to prayerfully consider what specific things you can do to accomplish this goal. Rise to the challenge.

Psalm 133; Ephesians 4:1-6

> *Have I then become your enemy by telling you the truth?*
> — Galatians 4:16

By answering this one short inspired question, you can pinpoint the problem. You have proclaimed the truth and people do not like it. This happens all the time. You may even have jeopardized a close relationship by telling someone the truth of Scripture in love. To believers, truth is comforting, encouraging, and sharpening. To unbelievers, it is harsh, hurtful, and intolerant.

For the sake of the gospel, the salvation of souls, and true church unity, you must not compromise the truth even if people disagree with you, scorn your conviction, or become your enemy. You cannot ignore false teaching under the guise of being nice. Therefore, continue speaking the truth in love even if it is ignored.

2 Samuel 12:1-15; 2 Timothy 4:1-2

'What, then, is to be done?'

— Acts 21:22

You may have the right doctrines and belief but have found that communicating them is still difficult. The best way to keep the peace and promote unity is not always evident, and many rumors may already be circulating about the issue or issues. You still need to have a plan, make a decision, and pursue reconciliation. You cannot wait any longer. Recall these words from the book of Proverbs: 'In the abundance of counselors there is victory.' Deliberate with other godly believers. Ask them for prayer and accountability. Even if your attempt to defuse the situation fails, you went about it in the right way. Be hopeful.

Proverbs 15:22; Acts 16:4

If the whole body were an eye, where would be the sense of hearing? If the whole body were an ear, where would be the sense of smell?

— 1 Corinthians 12:17

There is no superiority or inferiority in the family of God. You need every other believer, just as every other believer needs you. Yet we are not all the same. We have different gifts and functions. This unity in diversity is by God's design. There is order. There is divine placement. The body of Christ is impaired if any person is disconnected or failing. If anyone is absent, everyone is hindered.

You, too, must contribute accordingly. You are not called to be a spectator. Use your spiritual gift(s) for His glory and the church's good. Guard against divisive attitudes and actions. In no way yield to pride.

2 Chronicles 30:10-12; Romans 12:4-8

For if I cause you pain, who is there to make me glad
but the one whom I have pained?

– 2 Corinthians 2:2

Part of your joy and happiness is bound up in other people. If they are in pain, so are you. If what they have done causes them hurt, you hurt, too. But that should not negate your obligation to keep them accountable. They may need to experience sorrow for a season because the purity of the church is in jeopardy. God's goal is for their repentance. In knowing that all things work together for the good of those who love Him, you can rejoice and be glad again. But if they do not repent, you must not compromise the truth for a false sense of unity. You must always balance the call for unity with the purity of the church, both doctrinally and morally. Do not jettison core doctrines or ignore loose living for the sake of false unity. Being in line with God's goals for another person will give you more peace than doing otherwise.

Jeremiah 9:1-3; Luke 19:41-44

'Is not this the man who made havoc in Jerusalem of those
who called upon this name? And has he not come here for
this purpose, to bring them bound before the chief priests?'

– Acts 9:21

You have changed. Something profound has happened in your life. Your friends and family do not even recognize you. Your past does not seem to line up with your present. The way you speak, act, and carry yourself is different. Your words are edifying. Your desire is to live a life pleasing to God. What people now see and hear is contrary to your old ways. Your life in Christ has people confused, stunned, and bewildered.

Do not stop. Keep increasing in holiness. Continue sharing the gospel of Jesus Christ. Many people can fake being a Christian, but very few—if any—can fake holiness. Be holy. Glorify God.

Song of Solomon 8:5a; Mark 6:1-6

'Do you want to go away as well?'
– John 6:67

For some people, Jesus is not who they are looking for. They only desire someone who will fill up their bellies, say what they want to hear, and be convenient to follow. You, too, have the freedom to leave, to go off with unbelievers if you so choose. But also, like the disciples, you have heard His prayers, felt His power, and tasted His goodness. You have also seen His Word in action through others' accounts and through Scripture.

Truth be told, you know there is nowhere else to go. There is no Plan B. There is no other option to consider. Jesus has the words of eternal life. What a terrible choice it would be to walk away.

Instead, stay the course. Carefully proceed. Persevere in the task of following Him. Rid yourself of bad relationships. Set up some accountability. Seek friendships and conversations that will benefit your soul. Strain every nerve you can to remain in this blessed state.

Hosea 13:4; Acts 4:12

For what credit is it if, when you sin and are beaten for it, you endure?
– 1 Peter 2:20

God will not reward you for any kind of endurance through suffering, but for enduring through undeserved suffering. In other words, you will receive no special honor or approval from God if you merely do what everyone else in this world can do. You are called to be different. Yet you are not unique if you suffer for something you deserve punishment for. Many guilty prisoners, for example, serve their time and endure suffering. They have reaped what they sowed.

What is great in God's eyes is when you do right and suffer for it. You do not seek revenge. You do not complain. You do not turn from God. Rather, you patiently endure. You trust God. You forgive. What a Christian does is reject the natural inclinations, which shows their faith to be genuine. Then—and only then—will God approve your suffering and reward your faithfulness.

Psalm 34:19; Romans 5:3-5

> *'Is not life more than food, and the body*
> *more than clothing?'*
> — Matthew 6:25

Yes! Emphatically, yes! Do not be anxious then about these things. God has given you a life and a body that needs food and clothing. But there is a radical difference between possessing those things and being possessed by them. If your daily focus and pursuit is on lesser matters such as what you will eat and put on your body, then your life will lack the fulfillment you can only find in Christ.

Some people spend hours every week putting on makeup, shopping for clothes, and eating at restaurants. Yet they could not tell you the last time they spent a few moments beholding some of God's beautiful handiwork and how He cares for lesser creatures.

You live in a miraculous world, surrounded by His splendor. Yes, God still wants you to have food and clothing, but living in a world that preoccupies itself with them can easily rub off on you, even to the point of addiction. A far more excellent way of life is to pursue God's kingdom (discerning how to behave because you are a Christian) and His righteousness (seeking to be holy like Christ). Otherwise, you will quickly succumb to materialism, which will enslave you and cause you to be anxious. Instead, store up for yourself treasures in heaven. Concern yourself with your relationship to God. Jesus modeled this way of life for you. Look to Him. Live in the happiness He provides. Be anxious about nothing.

Joshua 1:6-9; 1 Peter 5:6-7

'Why are you so afraid? Have you still no faith?'
– Mark 4:40

You fear what you cannot control. You want things manageable. Therefore, you need to keep in mind these two inspired questions. If you have so much fear, what does that say about your faith? You should have no reason to doubt given all the things Jesus has already done. Yet you still need to find the underlying cause of your fear.

This question Jesus asked pushed the disciples and will push you toward resolving to conquer your fear if you answer it. If you are ever going to be free of fear, you must find its root cause. If it is lack of faith, then you will never be able to respond appropriately to a crisis. The mark of a true disciple is to have confidence in God. Examine yourself in light of this simple truth.

Psalm 20:7-8; Romans 15:13

*'Lord, how often will my brother sin against
me, and I forgive him?'*
– Matthew 18:21

You are tired of forgiving someone. You do not understand why the person cannot change. You know you are to forgive, that much is clear. But you think you have forgiven this offender enough. If you keep forgiving, worldly wisdom tells you that people will just keep running all over you and taking advantage of you.

Jesus, however, gives you a completely different standard. You must be extravagant in your forgiving. It should be limitless. If you start counting, then you are not forgiving as you ought. It is not about an exact number, which would be to miss the point. Continuing forgiveness is the key to good relationships and communities, especially because people's natural response is to start conflicts. Forgive quickly, completely, and often. Do not retaliate. Do not try to get even. Forgive the offense. Seek reconciliation.

Genesis 50:15-21; Colossians 3:12-13

*'And will not God give justice to his elect, who
cry to him day and night?
Will he delay long over them?'*

— Luke 18:7

You live in a sinful and hostile world, where you will often be met with disappointments and discontentment. Rest assured, though, that God loves you and cares about your needs. He listens to your prayers.

Believe that He hears them. Be on your knees regularly. Relief and justice are coming. God alone supplies strength and power. Persist in your faith. Cry out in your desperation. He will hear you and lift you up. Do not give up praying!

Psalm 88; Revelation 19:1-5

February

'Jesus answered them, "I also will ask you one question, and if you tell me the answer, then I also will tell you by what authority I do these things."'

— Matthew 21:24

> *'For who has understood the mind of the*
> *Lord so as to instruct him?'*
> – 1 Corinthians 2:16

No person comprehends the mind of God, and therefore, no one can educate Him. Even though you cannot imagine anyone making such a bold claim, many people still live (and even pray) in such a way as if they are able to instruct Him. Others pursue worldly wisdom, avoiding the story of the cross, and practically commit the same type of error.

Be careful. Do not become overconfident. Live in complete and constant submission to God's Word.

Proverbs 30:4; Romans 11:33-36

> *'What is this?'*
> – Mark 1:27

You can hear and learn many great things from a variety of sources. Someone's teaching may impress you. A great deed or something new may amaze you. But you can only find ultimate, eternal truth in Jesus Christ. From His first public appearance, Jesus proclaimed and demonstrated that He was the Truth. He spoke with unparalleled authority and power, and His deeds revealed that He was in absolute control over everything.

Such supernatural teaching and actions caused intense discussion among the people and a variety of emotional responses. You, too, should give Jesus your full attention. Desire to know Him better. Do not remain quiet. Proclaim the good news about Him. He has the words of eternal life. Let everyone know.

1 Kings 10:1-13; Acts 17:16-21

Is God the God of Jews only?
Is he not the God of Gentiles also?
— Romans 3:29

There is only one God, and He is the God of everyone. No one nation, tribe, or language has exclusive rights. Every man, woman, and child can have a relationship with the one true God of the Bible. Nevertheless, even with the clear claims of Scripture to this regard, some people and communities still consider themselves the only children of God. This prejudiced and unbiblical view distorts the gospel.

Therefore, treat one another accordingly. Replace separation with unification. Invite others. Enjoy fellowship.

Isaiah 55:1-7; Ephesians 4:6

"'Lord, when did we see you hungry or thirsty
or a stranger or naked or sick or in prison,
and did not minister to you?'"
— Matthew 25:44

Nonbelievers can address Jesus appropriately, mention the same categories as you do, ask similar questions, and be as shocked at a situation as believers can. A key difference between the reactions of believers and unbelievers, however, is the manner in which they know and practice the truth—in faith, expressed by loving others.

God in Scripture calls anything you do apart from faith worthless. The condition of your heart makes all the difference. For that reason, all the 'woulda, coulda, shoulda' responses will be of no help on Judgment Day. You must look to Christ, not yourself. Deliver yourself into His hands. Thank God that you do not stand in your own righteousness but in the righteousness of Jesus. Ask God to shine in your heart.

2 Kings 4:8-17; Hebrews 13:2

'And if you do good to those who do good to you,
what benefit is that to you?'
– Luke 6:33

The self-interested and self-centered love of human society receives no favor from God. Such limited love—if it can even be called 'love'—does not display the manifold wisdom of God to this world. Instead, the world does good deeds for its own advantage or satisfaction.

In contrast, God's love through His people is far more majestic and far more influential. Extending love and help to those who cannot give back is countercultural, but it reflects the attitude of God Himself. Such is the free grace and unmerited favor God provides us.

Take all opportunities as occasions for doing good. Treat others as God treats you. Be generous and forgiving. Put someone else's needs ahead of your own. God will bless you.

Proverbs 20:22; James 2:8

'Do you see anything?'
– Mark 8:23

Ask yourself this inspired question often and take it to heart. During the process of healing, it is worth taking a moment to reflect on what you see taking place.

Not everyone experiences healing in the twinkling of an eye. It is good to reflect on how you are growing through the healing process and what you perceive. Jesus can heal you physically, but He also cares about your spiritual progress in the process. Even gradual healing, such as the one that causes Jesus to ask whether a blind man He has healed can now see, can parallel your ongoing spiritual growth. Full restoration, just like full understanding, can be a process, and God is in control of the timing of it all. Be patient.

Jeremiah 33:6; 1 Peter 2:24

Was it from you that the word of God came?
Or are you the only ones it has reached?

— 1 Corinthians 14:36

God's Word did not originate with you; and there are other brothers and sisters in Christ beyond your local community. Indeed, the body of Christ is worldwide. Your own ideas or prophetic words might be good, but they do not replace or serve as God's Word. All the more reason for you to be in touch with other churches and believers.

Look not only to your own interests. Reach out. Mend any broken relationships. Help one another. Fellowship with one another. You are not doing well if you are out of touch with other believers in the world. There is a vast network of believers needing mutual edification.

Deuteronomy 29:29; Galatians 1:11-12

Do you not know that friendship with the
world is enmity with God?

— James 4:4

If you and the world are friends, then you and God are not. That does not mean objects and people in this world in general, but when they are in opposition to God. To God, worldliness is any area of desire, influence, or belief that disregards Him and His ways. To become friends with the world, then, is to demonstrate unbelief and commit spiritual adultery. The pursuit of the world's friendship necessarily makes you an enemy of God. Therefore, it is both dangerous and stupid even to flirt with the world.

Unfortunately, many people will label or justify their friendships and ambitions as godly when they really are not. They come from their own sinful desires. They merely want to put God's stamp of approval on what they want so that they will not feel guilty, while potentially getting broader acceptance in the world. Small compromises, though, lead to big downfalls. Set aside worldly things so that you may attain true happiness. Stop living for this world. Die daily to this world. Set your mind where Jesus is, seated at the right hand of God.

Hosea 1:2; 2 Corinthians 6:14-18

'Do you not understand this parable?
How then will you understand all the parables?'
– Mark 4:13

You may have noticed that some people are content to live in ignorance. They are obstinate toward any message or viewpoint other than their own. They only see things at face value. Granted, they would probably not agree with that description, but their decisions reveal their heart. They have chosen the path of blindness and indifference to spiritual things by not seeking the kingdom of God.

A similar—though different—type of idleness can settle into you if you are not careful. Notice, Jesus directs this inspired question toward His disciples. They want to know all that Christ has commanded, but they lack the commitment and self-examination needed to follow Christ fully and faithfully. Jesus' question encourages them to understand the charge implicit in the parable: they must join Him in sowing seed in this world so that others will receive the message of the kingdom and bear much fruit. He tells them that they are only able to recognize the reality of His parables because of the Holy Spirit's work inside of them as believers.

You, too, must join Jesus in sowing seeds in this world. Guard yourself against spiritual laziness and defection. Place yourself in His hands and ask Him to fill you with His Holy Spirit who alone can enlighten your mind.

Isaiah 65:1-2; 1 Corinthians 2:8-10

Was I vacillating when I wanted to do this?
Do I make my plans according to the flesh,
ready to say 'Yes, yes' and 'No, no' at the same time?
– 2 Corinthians 1:17

Sometimes when you give mixed signals, it appears as though you cannot make up your mind. Some people might even accuse you of speaking out of both sides of your mouth, or of being fickle and impulsive. Yet, your decision-making should not be based on the mood at the moment or as a matter of self-interest or for personal advantage. Rather, depend on God. Interruptions are merely reassignments. God is in control. You go where He tells you. Any changes of plans rest on God, not you. You might say yes to someone, but God may later change your answer to no.

Do your best to live, pray, and plan based on your relationship with God. Keep your focus on God, and center all your plans on the gospel, not thinking purely in worldly terms. What a great opportunity for you also to be transparent with people. Tell them your reasons. Create a solid track record with people so that they trust you when God calls you to change your answer.

Proverbs 16:9; Romans 15:22-23

'Did not he who made the outside make the inside also?'
– Luke 11:40

It would be foolishness to think God is only interested in some external rules or an outward appearance of holiness. God cares about the core of who you are because He made you. If you neglect your heart and spiritual values, then you are foolish and lack good judgment according to the Scriptures. You need invasive heart surgery.

Therefore, examine your heart (internally) and your ways (externally). Grow in holiness. Desire daily improvement. Find a method of accountability. Come up with a clear and doable plan. Get started.

Psalm 94:8; Matthew 23:25-26

FEBRUARY 12

'What is it that you have to tell me?'
– Acts 23:19

Some politicians respect Christians such as you and exemplify the great virtue of courtesy. Some even esteem and consult followers of Jesus, accepting their wise counsel. This inspired question came from such a politician in the Bible. He took Paul's nephew by the hand, led him aside to discuss some matters in private, and took proper measures to address a matter. Therefore, never underestimate God's providential plan and abundant grace. God's mercy can even come through officials and governments. Be encouraged. Be diligent and studious in case a politician asks for your advice. Above all else, always support all people in government with prayer.

1 Kings 22:1-12; Acts 26:1

FEBRUARY 13

For it is time for judgment to begin at the household of God; and if it begins with us, what will be the outcome for those who do not obey the gospel of God?
– 1 Peter 4:17

If you—part of God's family—are being judged according to your deeds, then think about what will happen to those who never believe God's good news about Jesus Christ. Since God disciplines you—His legitimate child—and deals with your sins to purify and strengthen you, consider for a moment what will happen one day to those who do not know Him. By rejecting the gospel, God's free offer of salvation, they remain in their sin and will be utterly destroyed. Their pain will be forever; yours is just temporary. Your pain has an expiration date; theirs does not.

Whatever difficulties you are going through pale in comparison to what you would ultimately go through if you were not a Christian: eternal damnation. In fact, in relation to eternity your afflictions are but for a moment. You will never suffer except in this world. Be grateful. Do not succumb to the danger of focusing continually on your afflictions.

Psalm 145:20; 2 Corinthians 5:10

'See, we have left everything and followed you.
What then will we have?'
— Matthew 19:27

You obey God, and so you think He owes you something. Granted, Jesus has promised that His disciples will not love God without rewards, and if they obey Him, then rewards will accrue. But the rewards are not necessarily those of a material nature. God expects us to love Him not for the rewards we expect or demand from Him. Instead, love God without limit—with all your heart, mind, soul, and strength. Do this not because you expect something good out of your devotion, but because He is God, all-perfect, all-powerful, all-loving, all-merciful, and eternal.

As you become a lover of God, He rewards your faithfulness, but that is not why you love Him. That is not what draws you into your spiritual marriage. It's not mercenary love: I love you because you give me things. It's not slave love: I love you because you carry a big stick and will hurt me if I don't.

What God calls you to is a child's love. Yes, there are goodies—the kind that last forever. Yes, God does expect proper fear and reverence. But you ultimately love Him because He is your heavenly Father. Keep your affections for God alive. Seek out His presence.

Psalm 23:6; 1 Corinthians 3:10-15

'Sir, you have nothing to draw water with,
and the well is deep.
Where do you get that living water?'
– John 4:11

Most people are like the woman in this story. She doesn't know the true identity of Jesus. She is ignorant of God's gifts. She has no clue were living water comes from, and her mind automatically thinks about earthly things (the well water) instead of heavenly ones (the living water).

She is not alone in her lack of understanding. The theme of being so earthly minded that you miss the spiritual implications of everyday aspects of life runs rampant in Scripture. For example, notice just in the Gospel of John prior to this question that the banquet master doesn't know where the wine came from, Nicodemus can't figure out where the wind comes from, and this woman doesn't know where to get living water.

God has filled you with a thirst and hunger that cannot be satisfied by this world, even if you keep looking for fulfillment here. In fact, it is foolishness to simply run around filling your mouth with things of this world. You will never be content or happy if you do. Every appetite you have will only be fully satisfied in Jesus. Go directly to Him. Enter into the joy of the Lord. Write down some practical steps you can take each day in seeking daily spiritual renewal.

Isaiah 12; Revelation 22:17

But I ask, have they not heard?
– Romans 10:18

You are not the only visible testimony God has given the world. All people can see and hear God's truth to some extent in creation. The Bible consistently confirms that God's glory and voiceless acts shine forth in this world so powerfully it is as if they audibly declare His wondrous works. Using hyperbole, the point of this inspired question is clear: no one is left without a testimony or abandoned by God. God provides many opportunities for people to hear from Him. Even though most people reject Him, God's offer of salvation remains universal.

Know that God will hold them accountable. Regularly come before God to intercede for them. Stay faithful. Meditate on the ways that God sovereignly governs every part of your life and theirs. Write down the works of God that you feel give the greatest testimony to His existence and power.

Psalm 19:1-6; Colossians 1:23

'Why do you see the speck that is in your brother's eye, but do not notice the log that is in your own eye?'
– Luke 6:41

It is all too tempting to highlight someone else's failures when yours are even greater. Granted, there is nothing wrong with helping someone deal with their wrongdoings. In fact, Jesus goes on to say that the reason you need to take the log out of your eye is so that you can ultimately take the speck out of their eye. But before you help others deal with their problems, you first need to see clearly by dealing with your own (often greater) struggles.

Don't overlook or downplay your sins. Admit that you have done wrong. Apply the same standard of evaluation you use for others to yourself. Pray to God for His Spirit to reveal your sins. Put down this book and go to anyone you may have wronged so that you can make things right between the two of you. Offer to help others, and do so with gentleness, but do not ignore uprooting the sins in your life.

Psalm 36:2; Romans 2:1

'*Do you believe that I am able to do this?*'

— Matthew 9:28

Jesus knows the answer to the question He poses: Faith is a key factor in everything, especially healings. He does not ask you whether He should do it or if you agree with how He will do it. Instead, He asks if you believe in His wonder-working power. He wants to draw your attention to the spiritual, not just the physical.

Remember that faith alone will not save or heal you if you do not know in whom you are putting your faith. Everything you receive is through faith in Jesus Christ, not just faith in the idea of faith. So don't place your faith in faith. Instead, place it in Christ. In doing so, you will discover the blessings and power of true faith.

Genesis 18:13-14; 1 John 5:4

'You will not speak to me?
Do you not know that I have authority to release you
and authority to crucify you?'

– John 19:10

Perhaps you know someone in authority who has a higher view of themselves than they ought. They pretend (or actually think) they can wield more power than they are able. Pilate demonstrates this well when he asks Jesus these inspired questions. Pilate essentially says, 'You won't speak *to me*. I'm the one who has ultimate authority over you.' Jesus, however, is not intimated. He knows God's authority surpasses all human authority.

You cannot read the Bible without seeing the truth of this. Take comfort. God controls everything. Even if you don't respect the person in authority, you can respect the office and position the person holds, as Jesus did here and elsewhere. Whether it is a president, employer, teacher, or an officer who pulls you over, you must respect that person's position and submit to their authority. Never forget that whoever resists the governing authorities resists what God has appointed. Remember also that God can direct their hearts wherever He desires. Be encouraged. Pray for them!

Daniel 4:24-25; Acts 4:27-28

> *Are they not the ones who blaspheme the honorable*
> *name by which you were called?*
> – James 2:7

Even worse than having the rich take advantage of you financially and hauling you off to court is having them slander your Savior. God has named you 'one who belongs to the honorable name, Jesus Christ.'

Your heavenly family inheritance is yet another reason why you should not show favoritism to the rich. They often walk in step with people who oppose fellow Christians and speak against your Lord. By doing so, they give outsiders the impression that God cannot or does not take care of His people, making their belief in Him hopeless. This is an affront to God and your faith. Rather have the world against you than Jesus displeased with you. Find and remember the Scriptures that show you how Jesus responded to these types of situations. Do not let money, worldly things, or the rich distract you.

Isaiah 52:3-6; Acts 26:9-11

FEBRUARY 21

> *'Teacher, do you not care that we are perishing?'*
> – Mark 4:38

Suddenly, you need a solution to a problem that is outside of your control. You panic. You do not understand why God would leave you under these conditions. You assume He simply does not care anymore or is indifferent toward you.

What your despair may reveal, however, is your lack of faith. Maybe your lack of faith is due to your not understanding the great depths of God's love. You are not trusting in God as you ought. You may not realize that God is all you need until one day God is all you have.

Pray and ask that the Lord will give you the ability to discern and apply this truth: God is sovereign over everything and promises to never abandon or forsake you. Cast yourself in His loving arms and trust Him to be with you even in grief. You are precious and beloved in His sight!

Psalm 89:8-9; Philippians 4:19

'O you of little faith, why did you doubt?'
— Matthew 14:31

Being certain of who Jesus is but questioning Him in the practical affairs of your life reveals doubt—what Jesus' brother James calls being 'double--minded.' Your problem is not intellectual conviction, but the perceived contradiction between your experiences and what Jesus asks of you. To lack such practical confidence in God during daily affairs is to have little faith, and such little faith does not help during harsh conditions or confusing situations.

God requires you to seek and trust in His supernatural provision. Exercise faith in God Himself. Exercise faith in His Word. Exercise faith in His attributes, for He is holy, gracious, loving, omnipresent, righteous, and sovereign.

And be grateful. He can still save you who are of little faith.

Isaiah 7:9; Hebrews 3:12-13

'Jesus I know, and Paul I recognize, but who are you?'
— Acts 19:15

You may be able to fool a person or community, but the forces of evil know the difference between an imposter and a true believer of Jesus Christ. In the original context of this question, a cover-up was exposed. The charade was over. The pretenders were publicly humiliated. Only because of God's grace did nothing worse happen to them. In fact, God took what was evil and magnified Jesus even more.

If you are simply going through the motions, then now is the time to repent and begin fulfilling your God-given purpose. Dedicate yourself to Jesus before it is too late. Be reconciled to God and to others. Pray for help in removing evil from your life and to live in such a way that you magnify God more.

1 Samuel 18:14-23; Mark 1:23-26

FEBRUARY 24

'Lord, will those who are saved be few?'
— Luke 13:23

You may wonder how many people will be saved—a few, a lot, or somewhere in-between. But Jesus isn't interested in giving you statistics or calculations. The way Jesus responds to such curiosity is to focus on the heart of the matter.

So don't worry whether the saved will be few. Worry whether the saved will be you. The door isn't very wide. The path isn't very broad. You will have to be committed and put forth an effort. You will not just stumble into the kingdom by chance. On top of that, God will shut the door one day on those who do wrong. After that, there will be no more opportunities for you or anyone else to enter. Don't wait to see what happens. Don't just assume you are right with God. Examine yourself regularly. Be on your guard.

Isaiah 35:8; Matthew 7:14

FEBRUARY 25

'How are you to escape being sentenced to hell?'
— Matthew 23:33

How harsh and intolerant a question this must have sounded to a bunch of religious leaders, who thought they were in good standing before God. On the outside, they seemed fine and people were impressed. On the inside, however, they were corrupt and certainly did not impress God.

Sometimes your thought process on God's coming judgment needs a direct challenge to alarm you properly. The hardest of hearts sometimes needs to hear the hardest of words. Being trapped under the influence of false security is a dangerous place to be. If you cling to this world, you will lose everything. To gain heaven, you must give up all of hell and cling to Jesus.

The problem, then, is not only about choices but also about desires. Going your sinful way and pursuing the pleasures of this world will land you in hell. Wake up and let go of hell while you still can. Do not just go through the motions or come along for the ride. Exercise faith. Live your life in this world as someone whom Jesus has saved through His wondrous grace and mercy.

Malachi 4:1-3; Acts 3:22-26

*Or do you not know that the unrighteous will not
inherit the kingdom of God?*

– 1 Corinthians 6:9

If you persist in doing evil, you are in danger of forfeiting paradise. This goes for everyone. If you think you are above it, be careful lest you fall. This warning is real. The wicked will not inherit eternal life. Do not deceive yourself. Do not allow yourself to reject such a warning. If your lifestyle is evil, you are in very real danger of eternal separation from God. If this were not the case, there would be no questions, warnings, or verses like this in Scripture. But there are. Your behavior is a direct testimony of who you belong to: Satan or Christ.

Write this inspired question on your heart so that you will be ready when temptation comes. Don't assume you are guaranteed a long life. How abruptly you may be taken from this world! Confess your sins. Purify yourself. Pursue righteousness, along with faith and love.

Psalm 37:10-11; Revelation 21:5-8

What then has become of your blessedness?

– Galatians 4:15

Something has changed. Something has happened to you. At your conversion, there was a sense of joy, contentment, honor, and righteousness by faith. You had an insatiable longing for God. Your heart was open to learning from God's Word. You were living out the resurrected life among brothers and sisters in Christ. Where is all that now?

Essential food for a saved soul is righteousness. Jesus said we ought to hunger and thirst for righteousness. Do you feel famished? If so, you need to return to your former blessedness, and advance in your walk with God. Rekindle your love and loyalty to God. Seek fellowship with other believers. Rise again with a renewed commitment to pursue holiness.

Ezra 3:11 & 4:24; John 21:15-19

'Why does he still find fault? For who can resist his will?'
– Romans 9:19

You are responsible to love God even though you are not capable of it apart from the Spirit's redeeming work. This enduring paradox in Scripture presents a real tension. Your limited understanding of this tension becomes, step-by-step, more understandable as you grow in the Spirit, but your understanding will not be complete in this world.

Do not try to speak where Scripture does not speak. Handle God's word carefully. Do not let what you cannot understand distract you from everything you can understand at this time. God does what He pleases and has every right to do so. He is sovereign. He is love. And even when we do not understand why He does what He does, we can be confident that He has excellent reasons for His choices.

Isaiah 29:15-16; Romans 1:18-32

'Teacher, which is the great commandment in the Law?'
– Matthew 22:36

You want it simple. Even 10 Commandments—let alone the 613 in the Old Testament Law—are too much. You want just one central commandment given to you.

Astonishingly, when Jesus was asked which commandment is the most important, He responded with two commandments—not one. We are to love God and love others. Both commandments together hold the top position. 'On these two commandments depend all the law and the prophets,' and are therefore the greatest. It is not one or the other but both that are critical to God's kingdom agenda.

Your whole life as a believer, no matter when or in what context, ought to be given over to the ministry of loving God and others—just as Christ did. You need God and others jointly. The interlocking back-and-forth movement between your time alone with God and time together with others fulfills your calling.

Allow the rhythm of the Christian life—the biblically based, centuries-old belief that time alone with God and time together with others are intimately connected and work in tandem to glorify God—to regulate your life. Follow Jesus on the narrow path. Do everything for God's glory *and* the benefit of others. Take control of your schedule. Change it as needed. Carve out time for both.

1 Samuel 2:26; Luke 2:52

March

*'And one of them, a lawyer, asked him
a question to test him.'*

– Matthew 22:35

'Who then is this, that even the wind and the sea obey him?'
– Mark 4:41

Only God can command storms to do what He wants.

In a boat with His disciples, Jesus has ordered the storm to be still, and so it happens. What is impressive about this inspired question is that it reveals a greater fear than just the storm. They are now standing face--to-face with someone who has divine power over creation. He is God! And that realization amazes them.

In a similar way, your anxiety might be because you do not know who Jesus really is. Your mind is not clear. Fear takes over. Nothing seems safe or certain. Yet Jesus is in absolute control. Be sure you really know who Jesus is. Keep in mind that He is God. Act on the fact that you are His. Imagine the difference it will make in your life. Jesus can calm your life's greatest storms.

Psalm 107:28-32; Romans 8:19-22

'For which of you, desiring to build a tower,
does not first sit down and count the cost,
whether he has enough to complete it?'
– Luke 14:28

There is always a danger in doing something in haste. First you need to determine all that is involved and what is required. Such is true with follo-wing Jesus. It is dangerous to just jump into a commitment to follow Him. You may lose social status or wealth. You may have to give up your time, career, or money. You may be hated by or separated from your family. You may even be put to death.

Being a disciple of Jesus is costly. Therefore, carefully consider the cost so that you are not tempted to quit. Get to know Jesus. See Him and His glory. Know why you are a Christian. Realize and be grateful for the salvation which God has obtained for you at so grave a cost to Himself. Look to Jesus. Keep looking at Him and follow Him. Never look back.

Proverbs 24:27; 1 Thessalonians 3:4-5

> *'Now, therefore, why are you putting God to the test by*
> *placing a yoke on the neck of the disciples that neither our*
> *fathers nor we have been able to bear?'*
>
> – Acts 15:10

God offers everyone the opportunity to be saved by faith alone in Jesus Christ, apart from works of the Law. This is central to the gospel. Faith alone is sufficient, even though saving faith is never alone. Yet people still test God by adding works of the Law to faith. They insist on some particular work that is not according to the New Covenant of grace. But adding more requirements to faith is both sinful and expresses unbelief, as if Jesus died for no purpose. It provokes God's anger because you are adding to God's Word or rejecting the sufficiency of Christ's sacrifice.

Take a few moments to ponder ways in which you may have done this. Address these dangers. Recommit yourself to doing better!

Exodus 17:2, 7; Luke 11:46

MARCH 4

> *'Who is my mother, and who are my brothers?'*
>
> – Matthew 12:48

Jesus' true family is made up of those who follow Him. Merely professing allegiance to Jesus is not enough. You must commit yourself to follow Him—to do, not just to see. Jesus makes commitment to action a requirement elsewhere when He says that whoever does the will of God the Father is His true disciple. Your allegiance must go further than the words of your mouth. Confession without commitment is not true repentance.

Determine right now whether you are His child. Commit yourself to Him as an obedient child. Dedicate your life solely for God's purposes and glory. Patiently await God's will.

Deuteronomy 28:1-14; Mark 3:34

'How do you know me?'
– John 1:48

Jesus knows you. In fact, He found you before you found Him. He knows your past, present, and future. Wherever you are today, He sees you. He is the one and only Son of God. As such, Jesus can see what only God can see: your innermost thoughts.

Realizing this, you should be encouraged. Jesus does not speak merely as a man. He does not see merely as a man. He is God in the flesh. No matter where you are right now, He knows you intimately. He doesn't want you wandering down the wrong path.

Therefore, He beckons you to follow Him. And one day, when He returns, you will witness and share in His final triumph. Consider afresh this glorious message. Turn to the Lord Jesus Christ. Never look back.

Psalm 139:1-12; Revelation 2:19

Who are you to judge your neighbor?
– James 4:12

Don't slander. You are not God. You are not the judge of divine law. You cannot carry out the sanctions of divine law. In fact, you have no business placing yourself in a position reserved solely for God, the final Judge. If you have been judgmental, you have exaggerated your own importance. Pride is your problem. Humility is your answer. Humility protects you from certain deceptions. In fact, if a habit of viewing yourself as superior to others is perpetual and is not repented of, your attitude casts doubt over the genuineness of your faith.

Instead, love your neighbor as yourself. Exercise exceptional care and restraint when assessing your neighbor. Avoid being overly curious about other people's private lives. Submit everything to God.

Isaiah 33:22; Matthew 7:1-5

What shall we say then? Is there injustice on God's part?

— Romans 9:14

God may initially appear unjust because He accepts and rejects people apart from their own merits or accomplishments. But the very nature of who God is rejects the charge that He is doing something wrong. He is perfect. He is loving. He is merciful. He is just. He is infinite. He is timeless. He is creator of everything and everyone and can do anything He wants with anyone He wants and be right in doing so. Ultimately, you cannot know the secret things of God. Mystery remains.

Take a few moments now to delight in knowing what you can: God is loving, merciful, and just. He will always do what is right. Realize that your faith, love, praise, and obedience are not based upon fully comprehending Him. Ground yourself in true humility. Recognize your limitations.

Deuteronomy 32:4; Acts 7:31

*'Lord, do you not care that my sister has
left me to serve alone?'*

— Luke 10:40

You may associate godliness with a certain type of demeanor, personality, or work ethic. But looks, acts, and sounds can be deceiving; and none of those things necessarily equals holiness. A person might have a calm, tranquil, and friendly disposition, but that doesn't mean the person is godly or even knows God. It is also natural to compare yourself with others, or to become frustrated when you think you are being taken advantage of or carrying the weight of everyone else. You may even find someone to blame for any disparity.

A busy woman asked this inspired question. She blamed Jesus for what she perceives as laziness from another woman. The truth of the matter, though, is that the busy woman's priorities were disordered. Her busyness did not equal fruitfulness. Her heart was distracted from rightfully adoring Jesus, and distractions—shockingly, even serving others—can be fertile ground for sin and temptation.

Consider your ways. Use your time as God would have you use it. Spend time with Him. Remember the Sabbath and keep it holy. Remove yourself from the hustle and bustle of life. Find time to worship every day. Keep up this practice with great care and watchfulness.

Psalm 27:4; John 6:27

For how do you know, wife, whether you will
save your husband?
Or how do you know, husband, whether you will
save your wife?
— 1 Corinthians 7:16

You are called to peace in the Christian life. Yet you may now wonder about your marriage to an unbeliever since you have come to faith. On the one hand, you hope your spouse will be saved as you continue on in your marriage. Maybe God will open his or her heart to respond to the gospel's call. On the other hand, there may come a time not to fight a separation if the unbeliever chooses to leave you, because you don't know if he or she will ever become a Christian if you hang onto the marriage.

There is no promise in Scripture either way. No matter where you might find yourself one day, you still need to pursue peace and exercise due caution. Model Christ's loving kindness, devotion, graciousness, and patience. Never rely solely upon your own understanding. Ask one or more trusted believers in the Lord for prayer and accountability. Be willing to be tested, even for a lengthy amount of time. Focus on Him.

Genesis 2:22-24; 1 Peter 3:1-7

'Why trouble the Teacher any further?'
– Mark 5:35

You may receive horrible—even fatal—news one day. People around you say there is no more need to appeal to God. It is too late in their estimation. Hope seems gone, as it seemed to be when a ruler's daughter died while Jesus spoke. It was not too late—Jesus raised her from the dead.

When Jesus is in a person's life, what the person deemed permanent is only temporary. Not all hope is lost. Even the finality of death does not apply if Jesus decides to reverse the outcome and raise someone from the dead, as He did when people originally asked this inspired question.

Your pain also has an expiration date. Jesus is still—and always will be—the Lord of life. Even if you are deprived of all natural resources, medical help, or human intervention, may Christ's most blessed words come into your heart and give you peace and confidence: 'Be not afraid, only believe.' Healing will come—whether in this life, or the next.

Psalm 36:7-9: Revelation 11:11

'How long am I to bear with you?'

— Matthew 17:17

The 'you' in this inspired question is not just you alone. Rather, it refers to an entire generation—one that is unbelieving and unresponsive; evil and adulterous; fickle and perverted. Since a generation consists of individuals, this question's application is broad and relevant. What prompts Jesus' question, however, is the fact that even the people closest to Christ lack the faith to draw on God's saving power. The outlook for the rest of the generation, then, does not look good. They do not want anyone telling them what to do, and they do not seem to think anything is their fault. Even down to this day, people want all the benefits of a right relationship with God but none of the responsibilities.

Ask God to pardon your failings. Be diligent in uprooting the vices in your life and planting virtues. Hate what is evil; love what is good. Grow closer to God each day. Keep in mind your purpose in life.

Deuteronomy 1:32-35; Revelation 21:5-8

Did I take advantage of you through any of
those whom I sent to you?
– 2 Corinthians 12:17

People make false accusations all the time. They twist things to imply that you or someone else cannot be trusted. It is important for you to question these types of claims. Ask yourself if what you are hearing is true or not. Ask others, as well. Even the most honorable and trustworthy people can be attacked due to misunderstandings. Be diligent to identify the schemes of Satan. Closely examine the facts. Come clean if needed. Do not let your peace depend on what other people falsely think or say about you. Your identity is in Christ. And if you are suffering because of being a Christian, God will reward you.

Proverbs 10:9; 1 Peter 3:16

'Do you not yet understand?'
– Mark 8:21

Even though you have had enough time to understand, you may have failed to grasp what Jesus is teaching you. Having seen and benefited from so much already, you should be able to grasp the spiritual meaning of what is going on. Not understanding Jesus' teaching reveals that you have only appreciated the miraculous things that are going on at a partial and superficial level.

Being a disciple of Christ should define your reasoning, knowing, and understanding. The essence of your mind-set, or thought-life, should be on the kingdom of God.

Reform yourself in your thoughts. Do everything you can to guard against self-centered worldliness. Ask God—who gives generously—for wisdom. Focusing on yourself will only obscure spiritual matters and leave you without true understanding.

Isaiah 26:10-15; Hebrews 3:7-11

Where is the one who is wise?
Where is the scribe?
Where is the debater of this age?
Has not God made foolish the wisdom of the world?

– 1 Corinthians 1:20

Where you look for truth and whom you trust for answers is the essence of these inspired questions. You live in a fallen, troubled world. Ever since Genesis 3, when humanity rebelled against God, people's capacities have been damaged and are no longer properly oriented towards God. As a result, people's skills are not properly utilized, and worldly wisdom doesn't amount to much. Those who appear knowledgeable in this world sweep many people away. Yet these 'wise' people are unaware of (or leave out) what God has done through Christ on the cross. This reveals their foolishness, and their wisdom is diminished, if not overturned.

The word of the cross renders all human wisdom as foolishness, especially because it is permanent, reliable, and effective. This is why if you marry the philosophy or thinking of today, you will eventually become a widow. The world's wisdom is fleeting.

Therefore, don't depend on or pursue the people with all the so-called connections, educations, or fortunes. Lay up your treasures in heaven. Fix your eyes upon Jesus. Make Him not only your Savior, but also your example. Point people to Jesus. He has the words of eternal life.

Isaiah 44:24-25; Colossians 2:8

'Who are these, clothed in white robes, and from where have they come?'
– Revelation 7:13

While some people may forsake their loyalty, be swept away by false teaching, or let the worries of life choke them out, God will clothe His faithful in white robes at the end of our world. They have remained faithful witnesses to Jesus regardless of the circumstances, temptations, and erroneous teachings around them. They have endured all by faithfully relying upon Christ's atoning sacrifice. They still devotedly suffer for their faith, whether it is imprisonment, poverty, persecution, death.

God promises to protect such people, His children. You, too, can remain faithful just as these people clothed in white robes did in their earthly days. Exercise faith in God's promise that for those who love Him all things work together for good. Rejoice often that God is redeeming a great multitude of people from every nation, tribe, and language. Victory is yours in Him.

Psalm 17:15; Revelation 19:6-8

'"This night your soul is required of you, and the things you have prepared, whose will they be?"'
– Luke 12:20

You may be working very hard to set yourself up for an early retirement with years of ease. But the only One who has authority over your life may cut it short. Whether you fulfill your obligation to care for the needs of others, God will demand you to give an account of your life. No amount of wealth can pay off your debt to God. If you lose your soul, then you have truly lost everything. Wealth cannot quiet a troubled heart or make you truly blessed.

God has given you a tremendous obligation and opportunity. Don't waste it. Put God at the center of your life. Start by making one change today that will help you remain free from ungodly distractions.

Jeremiah 17:11; James 4:14

*How then will they call on him in whom they
have not believed?
And how are they to believe in him of whom
they have never heard?
And how are they to hear without someone
preaching?
And how are they to preach unless they are sent?*

— Romans 10:14-15

This long list of inspired questions ought to inspire you to do everything you can to support Christian missionaries. At the same time, these sequential questions do not equal a formula that will necessarily lead to the salvation of everyone who hears the preaching of those who are sent. The main point is that no one can call upon the name of the Lord if the person does not know whom to call upon. We need to send more people to preach the good news of Jesus Christ.

Be a resource—financially and spiritually. Provide whatever is necessary. Support your local church. Support one another.

Isaiah 52:7-10; 2 Corinthians 5:20

'Are you also still without understanding?'

— Matthew 15:16

At some point, Jesus expects you to understand the meaning of His words and how they apply to you. You should be able to grasp spiritual matters, see the reality behind things, and recognize His voice, especially after hearing multiple teachings on the same topic. It is your duty to gain understanding. If you do not try to understand, God could take away understanding.

Stay focused. Be diligent. Trust and obey all that Jesus commands. Keep in mind, Jesus rebukes ignorance. Yet just as Jesus does not fail other believers as their teacher, He is not going to fail you. Be often at His feet. Always listen to, watch, and imitate Jesus. Then you will understand.

Proverbs 24:12; James 1:5

'How shall I know this?'
– Luke 1:18

There are times when you may be caught off guard by what God is calling you to do. Everything seems to be against what He is telling you. Your circumstances, age, other people, lack of funds, and other reasons cause you to begin doubting. You develop a type of tunnel vision, focusing on the obstacles, seeing nothing else. Then you ask God to give you a confirming sign.

God is not constrained by circumstances or anything else. There are times when asking for a sign demonstrates a lack of belief or reveals you are only thinking in a worldly sense rather than reflecting on God's power. Stop and redirect yourself. Place all your desires and dreams where they are intended to go: at the feet of Jesus. Reflect on God's majesty, power, and intimate involvement in your life. See the opportunities and take them to God in prayer.

Genesis 15:7-8; John 4:46-54

'If I have told you earthly things and you do not believe, how can you believe if I tell you heavenly things?'
– John 3:12

If you do not believe Jesus when He speaks plainly regarding what is right in front of you, things that happen here on earth, then what are the chances that you will understand when He shares things that are beyond you—that is, what is going on in heaven? It would be like jumping from simple mathematics to set theory. If you do not believe and understand, then God is not to blame. Jesus has properly and plainly instructed you.

From this day forward, believe Him in all matters. Depend solely upon Him for answers. Recognize that the blessing of eternal life is all about grace and rejoice in the fact that it is so. Remind yourself who Jesus is and what He has done for you.

Proverbs 28:14; Hebrews 5:11-14

'Who touched my garments?'

– Mark 5:30

Jesus healed many people who were not His followers. In many cases, merely touching His clothing, whether believing in His ability to heal or not, was sufficient for them to be healed of physical ailments or conditions. Faith was not a prerequisite for many miracles, signs, and wonders He performed or that people benefited from. Faith, however, does allow you to participate *spiritually* in the healing process. That was true in the days of Jesus and it is true today. Beyond the physical healing, a deeper-level transaction—indeed, a holistic healing—takes place only *in faith*. And it is far more important that you are healed, purified, and forgiven spiritually than that you be healed physically.

Complete healing is what Jesus offers you. Do not look to yourself or others for that. Look to Jesus in faith.

1 Samuel 1:16-18; Acts 19:11-12

Who hindered you from obeying the truth?

– Galatians 5:7

When it comes to the gospel, we are not talking about mere opinions or preferences but about the truth. This inspired question—not to mention the surrounding language in context—may seem harsh. Imagine someone who has been nice to you, who is widely liked and extremely affable, but who has the wrong doctrine or belief system. You cannot stick around. You must not jettison core doctrines even in the name of so-called unity.

You especially need to identify those who are stopping—not just slowing down—your spiritual growth. If anyone prevents you from obeying the truth, your spiritual life will not progress. You may not finish the race. Thus, it is imperative that you finish. The Christian life is a marathon, not a sprint. Examine your relationships. Avoid toxic ones. Seek healthy ones.

Proverbs 1:10-16; 1 Corinthians 9:24-27

'What is it, Lord?'
– Acts 10:4

You serve God. You give generously. You pray continually. You sense the presence of God in your life and are sensitive to the Spirit's moving. Sometimes God's presence with you is so overwhelming that you simply ask a question like this one. You quickly receive confirmation that God is pleased with you. God has taken note of what you have done and is about to allow you to enjoy more of the benefits of your salvation in Jesus. It is not because you deserve it, but because God is gracious and loves to reward those who trust and obey Him and diligently seek Him. It works. Stay the course!

Daniel 9:20-23; Revelation 8:3-4

But what fruit were you getting at that time from the things of which you are now ashamed?
– Romans 6:21

Before you were a Christian, your actions and character did not please God—for everything that pleases Him is done *in faith*. So given that your pre-Christian life produced no true fruit, do not look back on it as if it did. Remove those ideas from your head. Don't live in the past. Dwell in repentance. Desire to do better in the future. Be careful what you see, what you think, and what you touch. Draw closer to God and fellow believers. Leave the legacy of a godly life.

Ezekiel 20:42-44; Philippians 3:12-16

'How will this be, since I am a virgin?'
– Luke 1:34

You may be justified in recognizing a very real obstacle in front of you. You are trusting God and what He can accomplish through you, but you do wonder what the process will look like and how God will carry it out through you.

Thus, you do not ask for a sign. You just want to know how God will accomplish it—any additional information He might provide you. You are willing and able to accept whatever the Lord tells you.

In fact, your question might even reveal that your faith is more open to and confident in God's supernatural power (like Mary) than that of a pastor or leader in the church (like Zechariah). Continue talking to God in prayer. Keep on humbly submitting to Him and His way. Never stop trusting in His love and loving ways. Be about the work God has set out for you.

Genesis 17:15-17; Acts 9:1-9

Do you not know that a little leaven leavens the whole lump?
– 1 Corinthians 5:6

Sin is a serious matter. As each day goes by, the smallest amount of unchecked sin in your life increases your risk of getting a worse spiritual infection. Similarly, a little evil in a group can quickly spread and infect an entire community. Either you deal with the sin or you are in grave danger of being contaminated and dominated by it.

Reflect today on the gravity of sin in your life. Properly appraise it. Do not merely mount excuses: 'No one is perfect,' 'Others do worse,' 'It could have been worse,' 'I have it under control,' 'I've never done this before,' 'It's been a while,' or other such excuses. Create and follow a battle plan to help you triumph over strongholds in your life. Do not delay.

Exodus 12:14-20; Mark 8:15

'By what authority are you doing these things,
or who gave you this authority to do them?'
– Mark 11:28

The only thing some leaders know is that they did not authorize something or someone. In turn, they feel defensive and challenged—and they demand an explanation from the doer.

In this case, certain religious leaders heard about how Jesus had arrived into Jerusalem and the welcome He had received from the people. The leaders were outraged. They had not sanctioned what Jesus was doing, nor were they in control of the situation. Jesus, on the other hand, humbly displays His God-given authority and control and responds with divine wisdom. Mimic Him.

Ask God for wisdom in how to answer critics who oppose you. Be slow to anger. Let go of any must-win mindset. Seek God's honor.

Exodus 1:17; Acts 5:29

'Have you never read,
"Out of the mouth of infants and nursing
babies you have prepared praise"?'
– Matthew 21:16

Instead of discounting children's youthful exuberance, Jesus highlights it with Scripture. Jesus uses an Old Testament passage of newborns praising God and applies it to Himself.

This is a very important concept to grasp. Not that an infant can literally speak, but babies' wordless joy reveals the wisdom of God, which serves as an eloquent testimony. If infants and children praise Him, then how much more should you? Imagine the changes in your attitudes and even your life that will happen when you praise the One who created you even before you were born.

Psalm 8; Matthew 23:37-39

'Will you lay down your life for me?'
– John 13:38

We all make hasty promises. The excitement of the moment can draw out empty assurances of loyalty. Jesus exposes Peter's emptiness during the dangerous moment when Jesus asks him this question.

Jesus' question reveals much about you, too, and even more about Jesus. Jesus is gentle and loving, even when you make mistakes. He will never abandon or forsake you, even if you forsake Him in the moment.

Take this challenging question to heart. Meditate on it. Count the costs. Jesus laid His life down for you. In what ways are you willing to sacrifice for Him? Make your applications as specific as possible. Honor God by showing enthusiasm. Incorporate this aspect into your prayer life.

Jeremiah 32:40; 1 Corinthians 10:12

'Lord, shall we strike with the sword?'
– Luke 22:49

People are quick to take matters into their own hands. They are ready to bear arms at a moment's notice when they get angry. Jesus here follows the opposite approach by submitting to authority and healing a servant struck by a sword. He doesn't resist, fight, or defend. He complies. He lets God's plan unfold.

How excellent Jesus' response to the soldier is! Follow His godly example. Remember how Jesus endured and how patient He was. You have the privilege of being like Him. Thank God that His grace is more sufficient and more abundant than you ever realized.

Psalm 45:6-9; John 18:36

'How did the fig tree wither at once?'
– Matthew 21:20

God may startle you with how quickly He reveals His power and glory or how immediate the results appear. When you see God's sovereignty and power on display in such a way, it ought to stimulate your faith and increase your confidence in Him. You should also realize that Jesus confirms that you, too, can experience the same power of God in your life.

Recall and respond to Jesus' words: 'Truly, I say to you, if you have faith and do not doubt, you will not only do what has been done to the fig tree, but even if you say to this mountain, "Be taken up and thrown into the sea," it will happen.' Jesus is using hyperbole here to make His point about faith and is not daring you to run to the nearest mountain. Rather, He wants us to believe faith is a powerful weapon. Take His promise to heart. Ask Him for faith to see great things accomplished in His name.

Habakkuk 3:17-19; Romans 4:20-21

April

*'I found that he was being accused about
questions of their law,
but charged with nothing deserving death
or imprisonment.'*

– Acts 23:29

'Why put me to the test?'
– Mark 12:15

People can try to trick you in many ways, even with a respectful religious question. They will conceal their motives. They will hide their evil intent. They are not concerned with discovering the truth; they just want you to look bad, to prove that you are wrong, or to exalt themselves.

Satan tempted Jesus in the wilderness much like this. He tried to get Jesus to say or do something against God, as he will try to get you to do. Jesus will not be fooled, however; and neither should you.

Respond in a way that points to God. Combat a critical spirit by noting the good. Be committed to promoting righteousness. Labor to be a peacemaker.

Isaiah 7:12; Matthew 4:5-7

'Shall I not drink the cup that the Father has given me?'
– John 18:11

Jesus really did struggle internally with the outlook of being separated from God. But He never doubted or rejected the Father's plan for His life. Whatever God gave Him, He accepted. Indeed, His willingness led to painful, difficult, and countercultural outcomes—but they were all part of God's will.

Think through this inspired question in your own life. If God has called you to drink something, drink it. If He has commanded you to do something, do it. If He has asked you to go somewhere, go. Don't run. Don't hide. Don't try to find another way. Instead, be prayerful. Be humble. Be submissive. Accept your lot, and may you be able to say with the hymnist: 'It is well with my soul.'

Psalm 143:10; Acts 21:12-14

> *Do you not remember that when I was still with*
> *you I told you these things?*
>
> – 2 Thessalonians 2:5

The expected answer is yes. If you have had good biblical teaching, it has centered on the death, resurrection, and future return of Jesus Christ. You should be able to remember these truths if you have heard them often. They are the core of what Christians believe! They are not just concepts to bring out and look at occasionally. If you remember what you have learned, you should not be disturbed by false claims or when you hear false doctrine. You should be able to identify what false teaching is.

Reject anyone who teaches a false gospel. Note what the Bible says about false teachers. Watch, read, and listen often and with discernment and discrimination. *Deuteronomy 13:1-4; 1 John 4:1*

> *'Who is this?'*
>
> – Matthew 21:10

People like comfortable categories. But when news spreads about someone whose actions are eliciting mixed reactions, they want to know who is making such an uproar. Causing excitement and enthusiasm is one thing, but causing a stir is another. With all the noise, crowds, and commotion, people wonder what is going on.

Never has this question been asked of a more important person than Jesus. In fact, every person to this day should ask this inspired question about Him. Stop and redirect your attention to Jesus. Engage others in searching and studying the Scriptures about Him. Jesus' words will show you the answer to this question as it applies to you.

Zechariah 9:9-11; Revelation 1:17-18

'"Why are you doing this?"'
– Mark 11:3

This inspired question may be one you hear. Have you become involved in an action you believe is service to God but that seems too out of the ordinary for people who observe what you are doing? People may wonder what you are doing as a Christian. They may even ask why you are doing it. Regardless of the situation, if God has called you to something, know that He will provide the way. Whether God prepares a person beforehand, links you up with another believer, or chooses another way to accomplish His will, you merely need to follow His instructions.

Trust His commands. He is in control. His plans cannot be stopped. Follow His lead.

Ezra 5:1-5; Romans 8:31

'What will you give me if I deliver him over to you?'
– Matthew 26:15

You just read the betrayer Judas's question—one of the deepest and darkest questions ever asked. And to think that it still comes in many different forms today: cheated by a friend; exploited by a loved one; abused by an ally. Sure, it is always wrong to cheat, swindle, and deceive. But betrayal by someone you think loves you takes it to a whole other level.

You might wonder one day what you will get out of being a Christian. For whatever reason (and it doesn't matter), you may think at some point that it is in your best interest to distance yourself from Jesus before you lose out on something or someone in this world. Remember this inspired question at that time. Beware of the subtle danger of self-delusion. Die to this world and be clothed with the righteousness of Jesus. Do not be like Judas!

Zechariah 11:11-14; 1 John 1:8

'Did I not see you in the garden with him?'
— John 18:26

People are going to confront you about your relationship with Jesus the rest of your life. They will hear you speak, see where you go, and observe your allegiance to Him. This inspired question, as you may know, drew out a response from Peter that wasn't truly in his heart.

No doubt replying to the question in the same way Peter did is still a choice today. You may provide someone a convenient answer, an unreflective response, or a flat-out lie for some ungodly reason, such as present danger, peer pressure, self-consciousness, and others. Hopefully, if that tragedy ever happens, you—like Peter—will burst into tears and repent. You will come out of that present state of darkness and emerge back into the light of Christ.

Forgiveness is available. God is accessible. Turn back to Him in repentance. Never look at that sin—or any other sin in your past—again if it does not lead you to praise God and magnify His grace toward you in Jesus Christ. Remember it is a sin to allow your past, which God has dealt with, to rob you of your present joy and future usefulness.

1 Kings 8:33-34; Revelation 2:5

'How are the dead raised?
With what kind of body do they come?'
– 1 Corinthians 15:35

The resurrection of Jesus was physical, not just spiritual. Of course, being fully convinced of the bodily resurrection of Christ still leaves open the question of how. People may ask you a similar question today regarding people who have died at sea, been burned alive, or been blown up by an explosion.

There are countless reasons why someone may challenge your view of how the dead are raised. Yet do not forget that we are talking about a God who created everything out of nothing, who knows the number of hairs on your head, who made you in the womb, and who holds the universe in the palm of His hand. Certainly, it is not beyond belief that this same God can raise people from the dead and give them a new body. You can look forward to the day that God will give you a glorified body that proclaims Christ's redemption.

Isaiah 26:19; Luke 24:36-43

'Is it I?'

– Mark 14:19

In a great display of humility, when the disciples heard that someone would betray Jesus they did not start looking around or pointing fingers at others. The scripture says that each disciple began to be distressed and asked Jesus if he would be the betrayer. Maybe they thought their pride, intolerance, or bigotry deep down inside would ultimately cause them to stumble. Perhaps they considered whether their foolish ways would triumph. Whatever they reasoned, they examined themselves first.

You, too, ought to respond to bad news about someone in your life with self-examination. Judge yourself first. Take a careful look at your life, determine if you may have caused any of their distress, and then zoom in even more. Know yourself. Recognize your weaknesses. Go to God in prayer, asking for help to overcome any flaw that needs correcting. Love Him and stay loyal no matter the cost.

Psalm 139:23-24; 2 Corinthians 13:5

'My God, my God, why have you forsaken me?'
– Matthew 27:46

The urgency of this inspired question as it relates to you jumps off the page. Time is limited. Faith is more than just obeying some rules or simply hoping for the best without a relationship. It includes a dialogue with God, and He allows you to ask questions.

Despite utter isolation and complete loneliness, Jesus continued to trust and appeal to God. He never lost faith, just contact. This was the awful reality of the cross. The weight of the world's sin really did fall upon Jesus. God's face was not shining upon Him at this moment. A cloud really did come between the Father and Son.

Yet God the Father was as steadfast as God the Son in accepting the terrible pain of His last minutes of life on earth so that the penalty for your sin would be paid for. The wrath of God was satisfied in this perfect sacrifice. Like Jesus, you must continue to trust and appeal to God despite your situation and circumstances. In the end, your sorrow will turn to joy—whether in this life or the next.

Psalm 22:21-31; 2 Corinthians 5:21

'Lord, where are you going?'
— John 13:36

You cannot stand the thought of being without Jesus. His words captivate you. His actions influence you. His miracles, signs, and wonders amaze you. Yet you might too quickly want to focus on His destination before reflecting on what He is commanding you to do now. The answer Jesus provides Peter to this question is that Peter will later follow Jesus even to the point of martyrdom. Until then, as Jesus exemplified, Peter and the others are to imitate Jesus' loving self-sacrifice.

In a similar way, before you focus on His future whereabouts, He wants you to follow in His footsteps. Live the Christian life. Turn away from iniquity. Practice the spiritual disciplines. Lead by serving. Know how to handle yourself. Resist certain desires of your heart. Remember the words: 'Blessed are you who hunger and thirst for righteousness.' Set your whole aim upon righteousness—and you will be blessed.

Psalm 107:4-9; 2 Timothy 2:1-7

'Why do you seek the living among the dead?'
— Luke 24:5

If you do not see beyond the death of Jesus, you have failed to see. He isn't dead. He is risen from the dead! God's Word is true.

Believe the Scriptures. Jesus is Lord. Acknowledge often and say clearly that you believe in Jesus alone. Discover and learn from the Bible what is possible for you in Christ. Forget your past. Rejoice in the fact that you are what you are by the grace of God through faith in Jesus Christ. Go to Him. Look entirely to Jesus. He is risen! He is risen, indeed!

Psalm 68:20; Romans 6:9

'Why is it thought incredible by any of you that God raises the dead?'

— Acts 26:8

Raising someone from the dead is not difficult for a sovereign and all-powerful God. If you know there is an almighty God, believing He can raise someone from the dead is easy. Yet the resurrection remains a main objection to the Christian faith. Just like believers throughout history, you, too, will be challenged regarding your belief in Jesus' resurrection. Your faith stands or falls on this core belief, and yet it really should not be that difficult to embrace if you already accept the fact that there is an omnipotent God. The logic is sound. People may still reject the resurrection, but it should not be because of its being beyond belief that an all-powerful God could raise someone from the dead. Hold on to sound teaching. Do not waver.

Daniel 12:1-2; 1 Corinthians 15:3-8

Does a spring pour forth from the same opening both fresh and salt water?

— James 3:11

Your tongue and your maturity go hand in hand. What you say is one of the most significant indicators of your maturity and heart. In fact, your tongue is a window to your soul. What comes out of your mouth indicates what is in your heart.

As this inspired question makes clear, one spring does not dispense two completely different types of water. In the same way, one person should not say one thing and do another. Your life should match the divine wisdom you are teaching others. Walk and talk should match. One word or one remark can negate everything you have done, just as one chemical can taint the water you drink. Take another look at yourself. Cleanse your heart. Follow Jesus completely. The condition of your heart is at stake.

Psalm 141:3; Ephesians 4:29

APRIL 15

'Is it lawful to pay taxes to Caesar, or not?'
– Matthew 22:17

Your true citizenship is in heaven. Yet sometimes the concerns of human authorities and of God seem to be at odds. In such cases, you may wonder whether God permits you to oppose government interests. Taxes are one of them. You may have a very strong view one way or the other concerning it.

This inspired question, however, is not really concerned with the law of the land. In fact, the law of the land does not permit you to ask such a question. The real issue is whether you, as a Christian, have to obey human institutions. While you may not always agree with how the government uses your tax money or the motives behind the government's decisions, it is still your responsibility to pay your taxes. Yes, devote your resources to God's kingdom—but give earthly powers their due, too. Leave everything in God's hands.

Daniel 4:17; 1 Peter 2:13-17

APRIL 16

'Do you not fear God, since you are under the same sentence of condemnation?'
– Luke 23:40

Coming face-to-face with God's judgment, a condemned man, nearing his death, asks this inspired question of another condemned man as he realizes the intense hypocrisy of a guilty person mocking Jesus, who is innocent of a crime.

In fact, anyone who speaks against Jesus ought to consider this question. At the same time, remember that there is always hope. No one is beyond help. Even a criminal being put to death can receive God's merciful hand of redemption in the final hours of his or her life.

You, too, must look beyond your present circumstances and past shames. Find your pleasure and satisfaction in Christ. Look to no one—and to nothing else—except the Lord Jesus Christ. Depend upon Him for every breath you take.

Jeremiah 5:3; Revelation 15:4

'Tell us, when will these things be,
and what will be the sign of your coming and
of the end of the age?'
— Matthew 24:3

During the time of Jesus, people assumed everything Jesus came to accomplish was going to occur in a brief, unbroken chain of events. Having seen a few dominos fall, they assumed all the others would fall immediately, ending the world as they knew it and ushering in Christ's reign, their restoration, and God's ultimate peace.

Jesus answered these inspired questions the same way He would answer them today: 'Be careful. Don't let anyone fool you. Don't be afraid. The one who remains faithful to the end will be saved.'

Therefore, heed His words. Be always alert. Be ever ready. Don't be deceived. Hold on to the truth. Confess and repent of any fear. Stay faithful until He returns!

Joel 3:14-16; 2 Timothy 4:1-4

'Brothers, what shall we do?'
— Acts 2:37

What a familiar question! What a clear and easy answer there is! You must believe in Jesus Christ to be saved. Merely sensing your own guilt, or fearing God's wrath, is not enough. You must see your need for a Savior and embrace Jesus. You must repent and be baptized in His name.

Do not delay. Make your calling and election sure today. Be not unbelieving, but believing.

2 Chronicles 7:14; John 3:1-8

*Do you presume on the riches of his kindness and
forbearance and patience, not knowing that God's kindness
is meant to lead you to repentance?*

— Romans 2:4

It is possible to focus so much on God's kindness, mercy, and patience that you end up using His forbearance with you as an excuse for not dealing with your sin. 'It is not that big of a deal,' you may think—'God will forgive me because He is merciful.' God's kindness, however, is not so tolerant that you can continue your business as usual. Rather, it should motivate you to repent. You must genuinely desire and resolve to change your ways so that the same sin(s) will not happen in the future.

Pause right now to ponder the enormous implications of God's kindness. Repent where you fall short.

Psalm 119:41-48; Ephesians 2:4-10

For what have I to do with judging outsiders?
Is it not those inside the church whom you are to judge?
— 1 Corinthians 5:12

You must judge people. The all-important qualification, however, is that you must only judge other believers. This is not a new concept. The genuine fellowship of God's people has always included, 'I love you enough to tell you this in love.' Indeed, this is counterintuitive, because you want people to feel good about themselves. But you cannot just smile at sin. God is too holy. Hell is too real. Heaven is too precious. Christ paid too great a price.

For the sake of the community and of each individual, there must be accountability, transparency, and discipline within the people of God— lest we become like the world. For the sake of the gospel and the gospel community, you must correct your brothers and sisters in Christ when they sin against, or stray from, God.

Love them enough to confront and correct them instead of pleasing and appeasing them. God will judge both your abuse and neglect of this command to judge one another in Christ.

Be careful. Be gentle. Be humble. Be faithful.

Leviticus 19:15-18; 2 Thessalonians 3:6-15

> *Does he who supplies the Spirit to you*
> *and works miracles among you*
> *do so by works of the law, or by hearing with faith?*
> – Galatians 3:5

God's work is ongoing. He supplies the Spirit. He works miracles. All these facts are given to point you to the gospel message. God does these things when you hear with faith. The Spirit of God worked in your heart to bring you to faith when you heard the gospel preached.

Do not forget how your conversion started. Every blessing you have and enjoy is from God, who works miracles among you because of the Spirit in the context of your faith in Christ. You did not become a Christian because you kept some of God's rules. No, your walk started because God had mercy on you. And your walk continues by faith. Keep on receiving every good gift that God gives you through faith.

Isaiah 41:10; 2 Corinthians 5:7

> *'Why are you anxious about clothing?'*
> – Matthew 6:28

Consider this fact: Nature displays how God provides for the animals, trees, and lesser-created things. He has provided form, design, and substance. He has added beauty, wonder, and precision. What a refreshing vision of God's care! He has clothed with beauty even a creation as short-lived as a flower.

You can expect His care for you to be even better. You are the height of His creation. You belong to eternity. You are His child. You can trust God to meet your essential needs. God always provides what His people need. If you cannot trust God to care and provide for you with such basic items, your faith is weak.

The answer to this inspired question is this: You don't need to be anxious. You can be confident that God can and will sustain you. Don't just believe intellectually in His provision for you. Have faith. Believe that the God who has made you is going to sustain you and clothe you.

Psalm 55:22; John 14:27

Who is sufficient for these things?
— 2 Corinthians 2:16

On the one hand, you are qualified for things that have eternal consequences, such as sharing the gospel and being a fragrant aroma of Christ among people. On the other hand, you cannot adequately rely on yourself. Your adequacy comes from God. Everything that has eternal significance is beyond human grasp. Thus, you cannot rely on your own abilities and resources. You cannot just follow a formula and assume it will work. This goes for churches as well as for individuals.

Be diligent. Be dedicated. Be deliberate. Always rely on God.

Zechariah 4:6; 2 Corinthians 3:5

For who were those who heard and yet rebelled? Was it not all those who left Egypt led by Moses?
— Hebrews 3:16

Even being led by a humble person does not mean you will obey God. You may still have a rebellious spirit. The issue is not whether you have heard the truth or seen it modeled, but whether you have disobeyed and still do. You refuse the journey and thus reject the promise.

You are among other believers who have seen God's mighty works but refuse to walk the journey. And to think, you also have Christ!

Any rebellion is intolerable. Take care not to follow the ways of your generation and rebel. Do not harden your heart in rebellion. Do not ignore His voice. Do not provoke Him to anger. From this moment onward, submit yourself to God.

Psalm 95:6-11; Acts 7:54-60

APRIL 25

Who is wise and understanding among you?

– James 3:13

If you are a wise person according to the Bible, then you apply God's truth via good works. An intrinsic connection exists between teaching, wisdom, and good works. You must demonstrate your wisdom and understanding by good behavior in faith. Simply knowing facts, figures, concepts, or commands does not equal genuine faith or godly wisdom. Righteous actions, however, do reveal them. Even more, true wisdom and understanding prevent pride, self-interest, and discord. They produce humility, self-sacrifice, and harmony.

Examine yourself regarding how wise you are. Determine whether you are more interested in godly character or worldly success; serving or being served; glorifying God or getting ahead of everyone else no matter who prospers. You know what the right choices are—choose them and you will be wise.

Deuteronomy 4:1-6; Romans 2:21-23

APRIL 26

'How can these things be?'

– John 3:9

Some people don't want to think. They are lazy. 'Just give me the information,' they say. Or they think, 'How can this be since it doesn't make sense to me?' In fact, their questions often assume negative answers.

As this inspired question reveals, a religious leader named Nicodemus models these types of sentiments well. He simply seeks information from Jesus, but his questioning is skeptical. Nicodemus assumes Jesus cannot answer his question: 'How can someone be born when he is old?'

If you want answers, you must humble yourself, listen to Jesus, and follow Him. Understand the limits of your knowledge. This does not mean you cannot ask God questions at the boundary of your understanding. In fact, you should—like Nicodemus. But you need to do so with the utmost sobriety and reverence. Remember that you are approaching the Almighty, the eternal God. But also remember that in Christ, God has become your heavenly Father. Whatever your questions are, humbly let them be known to God.

Jeremiah 32:16-25; Mark 9:24

'Are you the King of the Jews?'

– Matthew 27:11

Sometimes you cannot explain the finer points of theology to an unbeliever. Jesus didn't with this governor, Paul didn't with Festus, and there are other biblical examples. Jesus merely affirms what Pilate asks and lets matters take their course. Of course, rejecting Jesus often involves more practical issues than theological or philosophical ones—people set their affections on themselves and the things of this world instead of God and His kingdom.

Be careful. Satan will strive to expose you to such selfishness, distrust, and disbelief in order to turn you against Jesus and His church. Do not yield. Do not waste your time and energy on matters outside your control. Pray that the world might see what God can do for them through Jesus.

Micah 4:12; 1 Corinthians 2:14

But what does the Scripture say?

– Galatians 4:30

Scripture applies to your situation. In fact, let the Bible speak more to your life than anyone else. Listen to God's word. Put it into action. Allow Scripture to permeate your life. If you want to understand it, you must strive to live it. Of course, it is not how many times you go through the Bible that matters; it is how many times you allow it to go through you. It is better that you repent than to know how to define *repentance*. It is better to be humble than to recount the stories about humble saints. It is better to internalize God's love and truth than to memorize verses about the importance of doing so.

Pick up your Bible. Hear what the Word of God says. Memorize it. Obey what it commands.

Jeremiah 15:16; 2 Peter 1:19-21

Who will deliver me from this body of death?
— Romans 7:24

You cannot see your face with your own eyes. You must use something outside of yourself, such as a mirror, to see what you truly look like. The same applies here. You may feel worthless. You may look at yourself and think there is no way anyone could truly love you, let alone desire to save you. You may even wonder sometimes whether you are just some biological machine gone haywire. Those cries on the inside express your deep longing for what only someone outside of yourself can do: to rescue you from this body of death. And the only person able to do so is Jesus Christ.

You no longer have to doubt your physical resurrection. You no longer have to feel spiritually frustrated. Jesus Christ is able to deliver you from this body of death.

Psalm 33:16-22; Colossians 1:9-14

'He said to the commander, "May I say something to you"?'
— Acts 21:37

There may come a point when you can no longer remain silent. With all due respect for people in authority, you have something you must share. You have accurate information about what is going on and need to communicate what you believe and can do. Sadly, people often base their judgments on hearsay or too quickly jump to conclusions. Therefore, be politely proactive. Take the opportunity to make known your testimony and defend the truth. Educate them. Ask God for His strength to help you act.

Daniel 1:8-9; Matthew 26:62-64

May

'Now we know that you know all things and do not need anyone to question you; this is why we believe that you came from God.'

– John 16:30

'Have I been with you so long, and you still
do not know me, Philip?
Whoever has seen me has seen the Father.
How can you say, "Show us the Father"?'
– John 14:9

No one—apart from Jesus—has ever seen the fullness of God, ever. Thankfully, Jesus has shown Him to you. When Jesus healed, wept, washed feet, and the like, you got to see a glimpse of who the Father is. That does *not* mean they are the same person—they most certainly are not. But if you have seen the Son, you have seen the Father, because God the Son reveals God the Father. Granted, you still need eyes of faith. But you can see the infinite goodness and love of the Father in the Son. To see the Son is to see the Father. To know Jesus is to know God.

Consider the practicality of this in your life. Jesus opens up to you the way to the Father. You have a relationship with the Father right now because Jesus has shown Him to you. Your search for God, truth, and reality ends in Christ. Praise Him. Invite others to see your heavenly Father through Christ your Savior.

Genesis 16:7-14; Matthew 11:27

'*Why could we not cast it out?*'
– Mark 9:28

'You didn't pray!' That is a short way of expressing Jesus' answer to this question His disciples asked. They had tried and failed to cast out a demon by their own power. It is all too easy to become confident in your own abilities. You experience some level of success without turning to God. You begin to feel a level of comfort that leads to a feeling of independence. Yet the truth of the matter is that everything you have comes from God. You have no supernatural strength, power, or ability apart from Him.

In the context of this inspired question, think about how the disciples failed because they did not turn to God in prayer. Then take a moment to realize that your prayer life—or lack thereof—reveals more about you than you may have thought. In fact, a day without prayer is a boast against God. You are essentially saying, 'I got this. I don't need your help.' Yet that is the exact opposite of how Christ lived, how He means for a believer to live, and how you ought to live. Therefore, pray!

Psalm 34:17-19; 1 Thessalonians 5:17

'*Why do you think evil in your hearts?*'
– Matthew 9:4

Jesus knows when your thoughts are sinful. He also knows that the way to your heart is through your mind. His inspired question here is meant to hit your heart through your mind as you meditate on it.

There is a big difference between grasping the truth and having it grasp you. The latter is the goal. It is not enough just to understand all that God's Word says and that Christ commands. You must value it. Embrace it. Apply it.

Where your thoughts are fixed, your heart is fixed. Sweep away evil thoughts from your mind. Labor to be spiritually minded.

Proverbs 23:6-8; 1 Thessalonians 5:19-22

'What is this word?'

– Luke 4:36

When you see or experience something you never have before, you often question it. You discuss the significance of it. Here, Jesus has demonstrated supernatural power, even over evil forces. This inspired question reflects the crowd's curiosity. Jesus did what He did by His words alone. No magical formula! No sorcery or witchcraft! No mere entertainment or illusions! That is what astounded people and still does to this day. Jesus does not have to conjure up some greater spiritual force; He simply employs the power and authority He already has. He remains in complete control. He offers what is good and holy to everyone.

Picture this goal in your mind: Jesus in absolute control of your life. Give your struggles to Him. He's the only One who can really do something about them for you. For every time you look at yourself, look ten times at Jesus.

Proverbs 19:23; Acts 19:11-20

Did you suffer so many things in vain—if indeed it was in vain?

– Galatians 3:4

Nothing you do has any value in God's eyes if it is done apart from faith. If you renounce the gospel and suffer as a result, your suffering means nothing. You must persevere in faith according to the gospel until the end of your life. Failure to continue in faith is extremely dangerous. It has eternal consequences.

You must answer this inspired question for yourself. Allow it to provoke you to re-examine yourself and repent where needed. Do not reject the Spirit's work in your life, lest everything you did and do will be in vain. Instead, focus on how God deepens and changes you through this trial or unbroken period of suffering. God is always purposeful. Fulfill your purpose in Him.

Psalm 23:4; Matthew 5:10

'Then are you also without understanding?'
– Mark 7:18

Jesus wonders if you will choose to understand His parables or remain without any attempt to understand them. Your mindlessness may be because you have become so accustomed to seeing things with only one lens.

In this case, Jesus' disciples only viewed matters with a ritual, ceremonial lens. Jesus focuses on the heart of the matter, though, and says that outward things, such as food and drink, do not affect the spirit of a person. Whatever goes into your body does not enter your heart and affect your soul. What is already lodged in your heart is what defiles you—lust, pride, envy, coveting, foolishness, and other sinful attitudes. From your heart come all sorts of sins.

Thankfully, Christ is the remedy. When you believe in Him, He gives you a new heart. Do not squander it. Endeavor to gauge your heart. Devise ways to measure how you are doing. Grow in holiness.

Isaiah 5:20; 2 Corinthians 3:14

'What are you doing, weeping and breaking my heart?'
– Acts 21:13

The weeping of another believer should break your heart. You—like them—are devoted to the Lord and are one in Christ. Their pain is your pain.

At the same time, you must not depart from God's calling even if your friends and family mean well in trying to stop you. You must press on. Devote your life entirely to God's purposes, plans, and path. It is your duty and calling. Stay the course!

Leviticus 10:16-20; Luke 22:39-46, 54-62

'What is that to us?'

— Matthew 27:4

Once some people get what they want from you, they don't really care what happens to you next. Whatever happens is your problem now. They don't care. They got what they wanted out of the deal. They show no remorse. They deny their guilt. Such callousness is common among unbelievers. They have their minds set in the ways of this world, and no amount of truth will persuade them otherwise. They continue flattering themselves—never realizing they are on the verge of God's judgment.

Beware of such people. Don't get caught up in their scheming. Forget impressing other people altogether. Give yourself entirely to God. You must!

Psalm 55:20-23; 1 Corinthians 15:33-34

'Can this be the Christ?'

— John 4:29

You don't have to be a theologian to tell others about Jesus. You don't have to be embarrassed about your past. You just need to personally experience Him and have a story (what Christians call a testimony). Nothing in this world matters in comparison to knowing Jesus. No shame, humility, or uncertainty should keep you from inviting others to Him. Most people come to know Jesus because of personal testimonies and dialogues. Even such deliberate and unassuming questions such as this one can stimulate people to search for the answer themselves, knowing that they probably won't stop at a simple yes-or-no answer. They will formulate a fuller answer and respond accordingly.

Just like the sins of the woman who originally asked this inspired question, your past sinful life can now be used for the glory of God. Never look back at your sins again. Talk often of Jesus. Show the world the only way in which its problems can be solved. Save as many as you can from the fire of everlasting punishment that burns forever.

1 Kings 8:41-43; Colossians 4:5-6

'Do you see this woman?'

– Luke 7:44

Jesus often turns to His followers who need to be encouraged, corrected, and sustained in their faith journey. Here, an uninvited guest shows up to an event. Making matters worse, she does not follow common social conventions and infuriates the guests.

Jesus uses this situation as an opportunity to teach an important lesson in devotion and how to treat all people with dignity. No one—especially a self-righteous religious leader—is above instruction. You need to see people through the lens of Scripture—to see them as God sees them and to feel towards them how God feels towards them. It is immediately clear that the woman showed more interest in Jesus than the leaders did. She looked at Jesus in humility and saw God's love and forgiveness. Jesus, in turn, accepted her and demonstrated God's love and forgiveness.

You must deal with people similarly. Go and love God and people more today than you did yesterday. Discover how to abide in Jesus.

Judges 19:16-21; 1 Timothy 5:10

What if some were unfaithful?
Does their faithlessness nullify the faithfulness of God?

– Romans 3:3

God's persistent commitment to you and His people is not nullified because some people—perhaps even most people—do not trust and obey God. God always carries out His terms of the covenant. God's promises never fail. What you cannot accomplish—deliverance, escape, salvation, and so much more—He can accomplish. He has offered these and many other wonderful promises to you in Christ.

Strive to make your home, workplace, and other spheres of influence a place where the cross of Jesus can be seen and embraced. Acknowledge your limitations and turn to God, whose loving kindness endures forever.

Lamentations 3:22-24; 2 Timothy 2:8-13

MAY 12

'Lord, are you telling this parable for us or for all?'
– Luke 12:41

Everyone is called to be alert—*or else*. Everyone should be faithfully fulfilling the calling God has given them—*or else*. Everyone needs to be about God's business today—*or else*.

Leave tomorrow's uncertainties and life's unknowns in God's capable hands. Live in the present. Focus on this day's bread. God is not as concerned about what you are thinking about doing someday as He is about what you *are* doing now. Be a faithful servant. Use your gifts, talents, and resources for His glory. Do all that God has commanded you to do. Waste no more time, for you do not know when Jesus will return or call you home.

Ecclesiastes 12:13-14; Mark 13:37

MAY 13

'Who will descend into the abyss?'
– Romans 10:7

The gospel makes clear the message of salvation. The spiritual mystery of ascending into heaven and descending into the abyss has been solved. There is no need to go down to the realm of the dead, since Christ has been raised from the dead. Salvation will not be found there, and believers will not experience it. Instead, Jesus has accomplished everything in His resurrection. He defeated sin, Satan, and death. He is risen. He is with you. He will never leave you or forsake you. He has delivered you from such future misery and condemnation.

Take pleasure in knowing that a heavenly inheritance awaits you. Thank God for it. Teach others about it. Find joy in it.

Psalm 16:10; Ephesians 4:8-10

'Why do your disciples break the tradition of the elders?'
— Matthew 15:2

People will question you regarding your beliefs. They will wonder on what basis you get your religious convictions. They will assume it should be in keeping with their instructors and traditions.

The problem, however, is that the people they look up to may be wrong or may be interpreting God's Word incorrectly. They may be trusting in human tradition, modern culture, and current trends.

It is good for you to examine the traditions you have received, culturally, spiritually, and denominationally. Don't bracket your thinking. Be like the Bereans, who examined the Scriptures daily. Hold your traditions up to the light of Scripture. See them for what they really are, and determine whether they are from God or man. Identify and correct any ill-founded practices.

Jeremiah 10:2-3; Acts 28:23-31

Now if Christ is proclaimed as raised from the dead,
how can some of you say that there is
no resurrection of the dead?
— 1 Corinthians 15:12

The resurrection of Christ is not just one detail or doctrine among many. It is the essential detail and doctrine of your faith as a Christian. God calls you to proclaim this message, not just study it. In doing so, you will hear contrary things to what you proclaim regarding the reality of the bodily resurrection. And even if just some people deny Jesus' physical resurrection, their denial is still a danger too significant to leave unaddressed. One reason why this is so important is that God is not removed or distant from our lives. In Him we live and move and have our being. Despite our mistakes, He dwells with us.

As difficult as it may be, you must deal with any view contrary to a bodily resurrection. Pick up your Bible. Observe what the Bible teaches about it. Respond respectfully. Display bold confidence in God's promises.

Daniel 12:2; 1 Thessalonians 4:14

MAY 16

'Why do you trouble her?'
– Mark 14:6

Caring for the poor is certainly a regular need—an important obligation—and requires sufficient resources. Nevertheless, the historic moment and beautiful act that prompted this inspired question only came once: The woman was symbolically preparing Jesus for His death as the long-awaited royal Messiah. Yet some people rebuked this woman for anointing Jesus with a costly ointment, allegedly focusing on 'the good'—helping the poor—at the expense of 'the best'—anointing Jesus. They missed the spiritual significance of what was going on right in front of their eyes.

Ask the Holy Spirit to open your eyes to see when unique spiritual opportunities arise before you. Remain aware. Even if you are not the one to perform the act, rejoice in it! Do not try to stop it.

Isaiah 57:14-15; Luke 10:38-42

MAY 17

'"Why then did you not put my money in the bank, and at my coming I might have collected it with interest"?'
– Luke 19:23

If you see Jesus as someone who expects too much from you, then it follows for you to be even more careful how you invest your life. Don't be selfish. Don't be lazy. Don't squander what you have on the kinds of luxuries that will only make you weary and useless to God.

Of course, the good news is that Jesus requires accountability because He has given you so much to use and gratefully enjoy for God's glory—time, talents, gifts, money, and resources. His intentions for them all are pure and trustworthy. The responsibilities He has entrusted you with are real and glorious. Be alert and watchful. Be a good steward of everything you have for God's glory.

Proverbs 13:4; 2 Thessalonians 3:10

'What do you think?'
– Matthew 21:28

Listen carefully and reflect deeply. Your actions will always speak louder than your words. It is better that you obey instructions after first saying no to them than for you to speak as if you are complying but then show by your actions that you have refused to comply.

It is time to recognize any inconsistency on your part and change your ways immediately. Focus on Jesus and obey all that He commanded. Determine what sort of change you need to make today and then choose to go after it. Regularly evaluate your progress.

Psalm 50:16-17; James 5:12

'How can you believe,
when you receive glory from one another
and do not seek the glory that comes from the only God?'
– John 5:44

The implied answer is that you cannot believe just in people; you will never see God's glory if you keep seeking human glory. Sadly, some people never take a stand to believe in Jesus because they are too dependent on being accepted by everyone around them—for other people can become your god.

By asking this inspired question, Jesus exposes unbelief. It's time to examine yourself regarding this question. Do you seek people's approval more than God's? Make up your mind. Seek God's honor. Desire His acceptance. Bring Him glory. Put at the center of your life the only One who has the right to be there, the Lord of glory.

Proverbs 29:25; Romans 2:29

> *He who did not spare his own Son but*
> *gave him up for us all,*
> *how will he not also with him graciously*
> *give us all things?*
>
> – Romans 8:32

God gave up His Son for you. That alone should convince you that your Father in heaven loves you. You have nothing to fear. God generously gives you all things in Christ. If you have Jesus, you have all things. All heavenly treasures are open to you. You have everything you need for complete happiness. Count yourself blessed. Appreciate your relationship with Him. Give thanks for blessings you have already received. Glorify God.

Genesis 22:9-18; 1 Corinthians 1:4-9

> *'Who will ascend into heaven?'*
>
> – Romans 10:6

Don't waste your time wondering who will go to heaven, as if anyone earns the right to go. Ascending to heaven is impossible for people to accomplish. Even more, it takes the focus off of Christ, who came down to us so that we might ascend with Him. There is no reason to guess, doubt, or question who will ascend.

Instead, focus on what God has done in and through Jesus. Only those found in Him will ascend. Abide in Christ. Be about the ongoing task of sharing the good news of Jesus with others.

Deuteronomy 30:11-14; John 20:17

'Do you know that the Pharisees were offended
when they heard this saying?'
— Matthew 15:12

Some people get unsettled or even angry when they realize an accusation pertains to them. When they are stuck in their pride, they do not like to be called out for their sin or be the subject of scrutiny. As you might expect, they try to hide their issues. They are the least likely to say, 'Help me.'

When you want to be in relationship with God, however, you must admit you are wrong. Ask forgiveness. Reengage your heart. Amend your life. Zeal for God's house should consume you, as it did Jesus. See to it that your emotions are controlled by a godly agenda. Grow in humility.

Proverbs 12:15; James 4:10

'Can anyone withhold water for baptizing these people,
who have received the Holy Spirit just as we have?'
— Acts 10:47

No matter who places their faith in Jesus Christ, they should be baptized. There is no good reason to delay, hinder, or block it. Indeed, no one should hinder what God is doing. God has granted them salvation and they have received the Holy Spirit.

Appreciate and embrace your spiritual family. Assist others in their walks with Christ. Band together with other believers. Cherish these things. Celebrate often!

Ezekiel 36:24-27; Matthew 28:19

'Can a blind man lead a blind man?
Will they not both fall into a pit?'

– Luke 6:39

Guiding someone without being able to see what is around you is dangerous. If you are going to lead someone somewhere, you must have clear vision. Likewise, if you are going to teach others, you must be teachable.

As a believer, you see clearly Whom you must follow. You know the end of the story. But it is not enough just to see Jesus and know the truth. You must also live it out. Reflect on this truth often. Conduct yourself accordingly. Be discerning whom you follow. Don't go beyond what Jesus has commanded. Aim to be like Him.

Isaiah 56:10; 2 Timothy 3:12-13

MAY 25

Do I say these things on human authority?
Does not the Law say the same?

– 1 Corinthians 9:8

Scripture affirms that workers deserve a fair wage. It is a biblical principle also embraced by the wider society. This concept applies to all people, including those who minister. You may question how much a minister of the gospel needs, but you cannot question whether the Bible permits them to receive money. In fact, God's law requires it.

The main reason for drawing attention to this in Scripture, however, is to drive home a different point: Christians should be willing to give up their rights when necessary or prudent. You may be able to point to a verse that permits you do to something, but that does not mean you always should.

Be discerning. Be humble. Count others more significant than yourself. View things in their proper light.

Deuteronomy 25:4; Matthew 10:9-15

'Then who can be saved?'
– Mark 10:26

The people who asked this question of Jesus might have expected Jesus to echo a common belief that a rich person was one who was in God's favor. Throughout history, there has been a widespread assumption that God must have bestowed His blessing on people who are rich because riches come from God. But Jesus' answer astonished them. He said it would be easier for a camel to go through the eye of a needle than for a rich person to enter God's kingdom.

If the popular idea of who is in God's favor is incorrect (which it is), then it seems as if no one can be saved. The good news, however, is that salvation has to do with the kingdom and household of God—not man. Where you are helpless, hopeless, and perhaps even penniless, God provides His Son, Jesus Christ. If you believe in Him, you will not perish but have eternal life. Remind yourself constantly of this truth.

Isaiah 57:12; Romans 10:9-10

'Can this be the Son of David?'
– Matthew 12:23

Many people see Jesus' power. They admire His feats. They respect His teaching. But just witnessing Him in action does not lead them to faith. Despite all His miracles, signs, and wonders, some people are more concerned about the political aspects of His coming. In Jesus' day, many believed that since Jesus was a descendant of King David, He must be fulfilling the centuries-old expectation of the promised Messiah as a conquering ruler who would save Israel from its enemies. As time went by, however, Jesus was not satisfying all their expectations.

Getting side-tracked by such expectations can damage your faith because you do not see God's hand working in other ways. Such disappointments are powerful tools Satan uses to produce frustration, anger, bitterness, and doubt in you. Satan can use similar tactics in your marriage, parenting, church, friendships, and vocation.

Remain aware. Challenge your thinking. Communicate with God.

Proverbs 10:28; Philippians 3:17-21

Do you not know that you are God's temple
and that God's Spirit dwells in you?

— 1 Corinthians 3:16

Behave according to what you know. Know that God resides in you. You are God's temple; indeed, you are the most sacred area in the temple. Therefore, live up to God's standard of holiness. Strive to please Him. If you only know these things intellectually, it is time to seriously consider the implications of who you really are as one of God's chosen people. Spend more time and effort in becoming holy. Keep in step with the Holy Spirit. Walk consistently in His guidance.

Ezekiel 10; Ephesians 2:19-22

MAY 29

'And who is my neighbor?'

— Luke 10:29

Most people assume that their neighbor is someone in their own community. But the lawyer who asks this inspired question wants Jesus to define exactly what 'neighbor' means. In other words, the lawyer wants his obligations spelled out and any limits specifically defined.

Yet Jesus reveals that the definition of 'neighbor' is not as narrow as you may have thought. It is not limited to people in your sphere of influence or close-knit group. In fact, your neighbor includes avowed atheists; radical Islamic terrorists; Mormons; Jehovah's Witnesses; virtually anyone. They are people to love, and therefore, they are your neighbors. Expect challenges. Gauge your heart every day. Consider how Jesus would have you respond.

Deuteronomy 10:17-22; Matthew 5:43-48

'Why could we not cast it out?'
— Matthew 17:19

You may get to a point where you feel pretty self-sufficient. You no longer rely on faith. You try to do it all yourself—just going through the motions and expecting the same results. Then feelings of inadequacy hit you. Your puffed-up ego deflates. Your self-confidence comes back to bite you.

The good news is that God will not forsake you. Recognize your spiritual poverty. Return to God. Seek forgiveness. Turn instinctively to prayer. Ask God for the grace to identify a lack of faith in yourself both now and in the future.

Proverbs 3:5; James 1:5-8

'What does this mean?'
— Acts 2:12

Like wind, the Holy Spirit's activity is often tough to grasp. Some people marvel; others mock. Nevertheless, you know better. The Holy Spirit is moving. God is at work.

Therefore, ask the Holy Spirit to awaken the slumbering souls of those around you who do not yet feel His presence in their lives. Let them hear you praise God for such spiritual outpourings of His love. Let nothing keep you from experiencing His blessings or seeking to understand His purposes in the present. Continue gathering with God's people.

1 Samuel 10:1-13; John 16:12-15

June

*'And when they had brought them, they
set them before the council.
And the high priest questioned them.'*

– Acts 5:27

Why not rather suffer wrong? Why not rather be defrauded?

— 1 Corinthians 6:7

Before any verdict is reached, you have lost if you have filed a lawsuit against a fellow believer. It is an utter defeat. It shows that you cannot endure a wrong. It damages the church's reputation before the world. Whatever temporary gain you may receive does not offset the eternal loss you will incur.

Do not live like the world, who always demand their rights. The world, where selfishness rules the day, sue for everything. Even if there are a thousand reasons to pursue a lawsuit against another believer, here is one that trumps them all: You are a Christian, too. No 'ifs, ands, or buts' about it. Your safety, your gain, and your reputation are not greater than that of the cross. Trust in God. Be a role model of godliness.

Psalm 34:19; 1 Peter 2:19-25

'Why do you eat and drink with
tax collectors and sinners?'

— Luke 5:30

Say you spend time with some people who are unpopular, people that others see as offensive culturally, inferior ethnically, or maybe even unclean ritually. The implication is that people will judge you for associating with these so-called 'lesser people.' It is not hard to imagine, since sinful discrimination exists in every generation.

This inspired question is asked by some religious leaders who did not approve of the people Jesus chose to befriend. Jesus' answer? We might state His reply in modern terms: 'I sit with those who call to me, not with those who don't.'

Consider His example. Show faithful love and compassion to others. Challenge, counter, and combat any unjust prejudice. Cultivate having the mind of Christ.

Proverbs 28:27; Hebrews 13:16

JUNE 3

'Could not he who opened the eyes of the blind man
also have kept this man from dying?'

– John 11:37

You may find yourself questioning God's love whenever He doesn't prevent something tragic from happening. You may even doubt His power whenever He doesn't stop a heartbreaking event from taking place. Both thoughts, though, directly challenge God's character; for He is truly all-powerful and all-loving. These were the same types of arguments people voiced when Jesus hung from the cross. If Jesus could save and heal so many other people, they reasoned, why can't He save Himself from the crucifixion?

With this inspired question about the death of Lazarus, you already start getting answers. Through tragedies—even someone's death—God displays His glory. No matter what problem may come your way or seem irreversible at the moment—even death—God has a loving plan and is in absolute control. Trust in Him. Keep on exercising righteousness. Look at the great and perfect example of Jesus, who said with His final breath, 'Father, into your hands I commit my spirit!'

Psalm 42; Matthew 27:46

JUNE 4

'Why, what evil has he done?'

– Mark 15:14

Even people who do not follow Jesus wonder why He was crucified—why such an injustice took place. Pilate, the one asking this inspired question, tries to free Jesus three times. Pilate does not see Him deserving death. Granted, he still had the authority to pardon Jesus, but willingly refused. But the people's minds were made up and no number of questions was going to change their resolve. In fact, they never answer Pilate's question; they merely yell, 'Crucify Him!'

Take time to consider here how evil may appear to triumph at times. Bad people look as if they are winning. God appears to be absent. Yet the reality is that God is in absolute control. Evil will be utterly defeated. Jesus is thoroughly victorious! You, too, are victorious in Christ. Give your struggles to Jesus. Rest in Him.

Deuteronomy 21:22-23; Galatians 3:13-14

'Did you receive the Holy Spirit when you believed?'

— Acts 19:2

If you do not know if someone has the Holy Spirit in their life, ask. Many reasons could lead you to believe otherwise, but you will not know until you ask. Do not just assume everyone is saved because they are around you or the church. You will be surprised how many people do not know or have not followed the basic tenets of the faith, nor do they have the Holy Spirit in their life. Do not be afraid. Do it from love, in love, and for love.

Zechariah 12:10; Galatians 3:2, 14

'Then what shall I do with Jesus who is called Christ?'

— Matthew 27:22

It is not that the people were supportive of someone else and indifferent toward Jesus. Even after many years of healing and teaching people, performing all sorts of signs, miracles, and wonders, He stood condemned by recognized leaders and a multitude of people who knew Him. How easy it is for fickle people to change their mind about Jesus because of peer pressure or the culture around them! The very people who had seen Jesus' miracles were yelling, 'Crucify Him!'

Like the crowds condemning Jesus, many people today are anti-Jesus. Antagonism toward Jesus typically happens when one's faith—your faith—may be put to the test. Take time to examine yourself thoroughly. Attend to your faith. Pay attention to it. Don't deceive or flatter yourself. Recommit to Christ. Renew your promise of loyalty to Him. Find out from the Scriptures what you should be seeking, loving, and hating. Implement it. Practice it. Keep your commitment.

Isaiah 53; John 12:44-50

'Why do you call me "Lord, Lord," and not do what I tell you?'

— Luke 6:46

Take seriously Jesus' question here. Even if you recognize the authority of Jesus and call Him Lord, being a follower of Jesus is meaningless unless you obey Him. You cannot bypass obedience and have either a close relationship with God or a successful prayer life. Disobedience will devastate you now and forevermore.

Notice that Jesus does not say you need to do what God says, but what Jesus Himself tells you. That is because Jesus is God; the second person of the Trinity. As you remember that discipleship is a matter of obedience, keep in mind that that obedience is to a triune God. Build your life around His Word. Apply it to every aspect of your life. Take time now to evaluate how you are doing. Develop discipline. Follow through.

Isaiah 1:2; Galatians 6:7

JUNE 8

For what partnership has righteousness with lawlessness? Or what fellowship has light with darkness?

— 2 Corinthians 6:14

'None whatsoever,' is the answer. You must quit playing with fire! You need to get away from your old ways. Avoid certain people. You are now reconciled to God. You cannot compromise anymore—not theologically, socially, or in any other way. It is inappropriate and unwise for you to maintain your old values and ways. It is the difference between light and darkness; Christ and Satan; believer and unbeliever; God and idols. Your goals are now different. Your activities are now different. Your friendships are now different. Your whole life is now different. Saying no to the world does not make you any less of a man or woman. Do not be like the prodigal son, feeding pigs, when your new life has spiritual food that satisfies. Discern the messes and recognize possible future unintended consequences ahead of time that can result from these types of relationships.

Proverbs 13:20; 1 Corinthians 15:33

Do you not know that all of us who have been baptized into Christ Jesus were baptized into his death?

— Romans 6:3

Do not forget that your baptism joined you with Jesus. A spiritual reality took place at your baptism. You were not merely identified with the person of Jesus Christ, but specifically with His death and resurrection. Your physical and tangible act of baptism symbolizes His physical and tangible death and resurrection. They are both historical facts.

In its simplest reality, the divine act of uniting you with Christ in baptism supernaturally enables you to walk in newness of life: reaching out to those who are neglected, treating all people with dignity, helping others succeed, feeding the hungry, visiting widows and orphans, and other godly practices. Christ's righteousness should characterize your new spiritual life. He gives us new life in Himself so that we might live as He lived. The two go together.

You are now a new creation, with a new heart. Affirm this truth today and live accordingly.

Leviticus 8:5-6; Galatians 3:27

"'Master, did you not sow good seed in your field? How then does it have weeds?'"

— Matthew 13:27

You may look out into this world and even into the church and be surprised by how many weeds you see. This may cause questions to pop into your mind or leave you with an unhealthy curiosity as to what God is doing.

Fortunately, someone else has already asked Jesus what is going on. They questioned whether God had made a mistake or what the source of the poisonous weeds was. It was a mystery to them. But Jesus confirms that people of all kinds will hear the gospel. Some will respond and grow; others will not.

Therefore, arm yourself with patience. Extend charity to others. Do not let negligence on your part ruin relationships. Let love increasingly characterize your interactions with others.

Psalm 73; 2 Timothy 2:14-26

'Was it not necessary that the Christ should suffer these things and enter into his glory?'

– Luke 24:26

Jesus' death was not the end of His life or the conclusion of God's story. Rather, His suffering was necessary in the outworking of God's redemptive plan.

By extension, your undeserved suffering might not make sense right now but it is all necessary. God is doing things in your life that at some point you will see in a new light. Recall and consider the words that Paul and Barnabas told Christians in order to strengthen and encourage them: 'through many tribulations we must enter the kingdom of God.'

Therefore, endure trials. Do not be anxious. Fear nothing. Keep on moving forward. Suffering demonstrates God's power through your weakness. He—who promised to never leave nor forsake you—is loving, merciful, and just. Be able to say today with Christ, 'Not my will, but yours be done.'

Psalm 22; 1 Peter 2:24

JUNE 12

What good is it, my brothers, if someone says he has faith but does not have works? Can that faith save him?

– James 2:14

The point of the inspired question is not to diminish faith in any way, but rather to highlight the false notion that *every* type of faith can save someone. A true profession of faith is never alone, devoid of a changed life and good works.

There is no contradiction. Faith alone saves, but saving faith is never alone. Where there is true salvation, there is real fruit. If there is no fruit, there is no proof that you are a disciple of God. If you have been born again, you are oriented differently than when you did not have the Holy Spirit. All the more, claiming to have faith is not the same as having faith. Inactive faith equals no faith. Take time to evaluate your life. Be obedient. Let others work beside you so that they can see your faith in action.

Leviticus 19:1-2; Hebrews 12:12-14

'May we know what this new teaching is that you are presenting?'
– Acts 17:19

Some people refuse to hear new and challenging words. Other people thrive on them. Instead of always speaking in terms everyone already knows, sometimes it is beneficial to use language and concepts they have never heard. For that reason, do not always think you need to 'dumb down' the gospel message or over-translate God's inspired Word. Yes, you need to be accurate, clear, and simple—but do not be afraid to offer a challenge. Some people get interested when they hear a truth they have never heard. They want to hear more of the truth.

Pray regularly for discernment on how to plant and water the seeds you are sowing. Always trust in God for the growth.

Psalm 119:97-104; Mark 1:27

'Good Teacher, what must I do to inherit eternal life?'
– Mark 10:17

Recall the first time you embarked on a spiritual journey in search for eternal life. Ultimately, you were pursuing the answer to this inspired question. Maybe you thought there was something you must do to earn life after death. Indeed, every religion that believes in a next world provides you with a specific answer of what you must do to inherit it, except for Christianity.

Inheriting eternal life is not about something you do. It is all about who you love and why. In fact, your heart will be restless until it finds its rest in the only correct answer to the question above: Believe in God's redeeming work through Jesus Christ.

Faith that saves involves your affections being oriented to God through Christ by means of the Holy Spirit. The most important thing is the orientation of your soul—where your allegiance is. Get away for a time of personal reflection and evaluation. Ponder. Think hard. Talk to yourself about your faith. Question yourself about your faith. Remind yourself of your faith. Pray a prayer of commitment. Allow God to impress on your heart who you are as a Christian. Be at peace.

Psalm 14:2-3; Romans 3:21-26

'Are you able to drink the cup that I am to drink?'
— Matthew 20:22

Pause for a moment. Really reflect upon your answer to Jesus' question so you can benefit from it. In reality, you are much weaker than you think. If you really understood the implications of all you ask God for, you probably would not ask for so much. Have you ever thought that maybe God's severest judgments on you are giving you exactly what you ask for? The main problem is that you do not ask for the right things or with the right motives. Being so quick to ask for things is careless.

Examine your thoughts, motivations, words, and actions. Contemplate your prayers. Show yourself to be a true follower of Jesus by following His example. Be a servant leader. Make sure you do not forsake God. Patiently bear all trials for the love of Christ.

Psalm 34:19-22; James 1:2-4

'What things?'
— Luke 24:19

Jesus wants to hear your thoughts. He wants to know whether you really understand the things that are going on around you, their significance, and how they all fit together in God's divine plan.

Perhaps you just know what everyone else knows and are unable to grasp God's purpose, plan, and design as yet. Whatever the case, spend time with Jesus. Share your observations, interpretations, and applications with Him. Meditate on and realize God's glorious purposes for you in Christ. Share in the bread of life. Grow in knowledge.

Isaiah 11; Matthew 21:11

'This is a hard saying; who can listen to it?'
– John 6:60

Listen in. When people don't like something, they often complain. It is not that the truth is vague or unspecific. They simply do not like what they hear. It is not the saying that is hard, but their hearts. That is why the clearest truths are often the hardest to swallow.

Seriously consider what reactions to the truth have been snares to you. Exhort yourself. Do not be stubborn when you hear God's Word. Be open and teachable. Do not accept half-truths. Submit to all that Christ has commanded. Never grumble or complain against it. Shut the door to all such ungodliness. The Christian life is too glorious and wonderful to be easy.

Proverbs 18:2; 1 Corinthians 2:13-14

'Why are you discussing the fact that you have no bread?
Do you not yet perceive or understand?
Are your hearts hardened?
Having eyes do you not see, and having
ears do you not hear?
And do you not remember?'
– Mark 8:17-18

This litany of inspired questions points to one major problem: spiritual blindness. Spiritual enlightenment typically occurs when several attributes work in harmony together: perceiving, understanding, seeing, hearing, and remembering. Yet Jesus recognizes that His disciples do not yet see with their spiritual eyes. Jesus rebukes His disciples for their lack of spiritual awareness. They appear no better off than unbelievers who are not following Jesus.

They needed to overcome spiritual blindness. And perhaps so do you. One way to do so is to maintain a heavenly mindset. Look to Jesus. Remember God's past actions. Pray for the eyes of your heart to see things from a godly perspective.

Jeremiah 5:21-25; Matthew 13:14-15

But now that you have come to know God, or rather to be known by God, how can you turn back again to the weak and worthless elementary principles of the world, whose slaves you want to be once more?

— Galatians 4:9

You have been set free. You are now in a safer place. The Creator of the universe knows you. You have experienced such extravagant grace. It is completely irrational, utterly foolish, and absolutely absurd for you to turn away. To turn away from Who is best to what is worst is simply unwise. You are exchanging freedom for bondage; liberty for slavery. Your old way led to destruction.

Therefore, maintain a lifestyle of devotion and worship to God. Develop your inner self by renouncing all that is worthless in this world. A godly life will give you more joy than the weak principles of this world. Give yourself to God and His ways.

Isaiah 43:18-19; 2 Peter 2:20-22

Shall we not much more be subject
to the Father of spirits and live?
— Hebrews 12:9

Without God's direction and discipline, your soul will weaken. When your soul weakens, it also darkens. When it is weak and dark, you will have no comfort and peace. On the contrary, divine discipline results in life—and life abundantly with Him.

Your attitude toward God's discipline ought to be that of respect, gratitude, and obedience. By accepting God's discipline with an open heart, you will stop feeling resentful and your soul will find peace and quiet. This quietness will enable you to enjoy your life more fully, respond to God more appropriately, and live life eternally. To have peace with God and strength to walk before Him is to live according to the New Covenant of grace. God alone reserves the right to speak everlasting peace. Wait for Him to release your conscience and speak peace to your soul. Resist the tendency to quickly—all too quickly—speak peace to yourself before you have actually dealt with your sin. That type of peace—forgiving yourself without repenting of sin and seeking God's forgiveness—is not from God and can actually harden you further.

Proverbs 3:11-12; Ephesians 3:14-21

JUNE 21

'Do you think that I cannot appeal to my Father, and he will
at once send me more than twelve legions of angels?'
– Matthew 26:53

Jesus knows His purpose and calling. He will not waver, even if it is in His power to do so. Obedience to the Father is of utmost importance.

In the same way, you do not need to fear people when you have God as your Father. You have far more at your disposal than mere mortals or human weapons. God Almighty, Maker of heaven and earth, can intervene. Countless angels are available to help at His command.

Model, then, Jesus' life of trust and obedience. Ask God to reveal what you should do in each situation to best promote His glory. Be not anxious. Trust God more than you fear humanity.

Isaiah 8:11-15; Luke 12:4-7

JUNE 22

'If then you have not been faithful in the unrighteous
wealth, who will entrust to you the true riches?'
– Luke 16:11

You need to face this inspired question. Face it with absolute honesty. Jesus wants you to see that there is a connection between earth and heaven. The way you use your possessions on earth indicates whether you can be trusted with heavenly wealth.

Granted, wealth can provide you with some temporal physical things: food on the table (yet not the fellowship around it); jewelry (but not the love that ought to come with it); a house (but not what makes that house a home). Material goods cannot save you from death. They cannot be equated with wisdom. They don't make you respectable—for even a thief can wear a business suit.

Therefore, be careful to observe this rebuke and understand what Jesus is saying. Consider your trustworthiness in things both large and small. Go back, examine yourself, and realize the truth about yourself. Rise up and press on by looking to Jesus.

Proverbs 8:18-19; Revelation 3:17-22

'*What do you want?*'
– Matthew 20:21

Deep down in our sinful nature, we desire prestige. We want fame. We covet celebrity status. If given the opportunity, we even trust in our ability to do whatever it takes to get it.

Jesus uses this inspired question to reveal that the simple request for highest honors may not be as glamorous as it sounds, especially when only viewed from a human perspective. You are merely thinking in terms of glory and power, when in reality, achieving honor, fame, or wealth involves a lot of hard work and suffering.

Imagine right now that Jesus stands before you. Meditate on the thoughts that come to your mind. Consider the great spiritual blessings you have and the emptiness of the earthly things you want. Whatever you lack, if you are godly, is very small compared to what you have. Put away all vanity. Establish godly priorities. Be ready to suffer if you want to have victory.

Proverbs 16:2; Luke 23:39-43

'*What then did you go out to see? A man dressed in soft clothing?*'
– Luke 7:25

'You did not go out to the middle of nowhere to see how a homeless man was dressed. The reason you went out there was because of the words John the Baptist was sharing. He had a divine message, and that message drew people.'

That is how we might rephrase Jesus' questions. Jesus asked the questions in order to lead the crowd into recognizing John's purpose in announcing the gospel of the kingdom of God and in declaring God's plan for redemption.

Granted, not everyone agreed with John's message or classification as a prophet. Yet therein lies the reason Jesus asked and asks today this inspired question—to determine what you think and how you perceive these events. Do not merely repeat answers you have heard. Endeavor to grow in knowledge. Steep yourself in the Holy Scriptures.

2 Kings 1:7-8; Matthew 3:4

> *Do you not know that your body is a temple*
> *of the Holy Spirit within you,*
> *whom you have from God?*
> — 1 Corinthians 6:19

Your body is included in the redemptive work of Christ. It is no mere accessory to the soul. Both body and soul are vital for your complete happiness and well-being. Therefore, you must glorify God in your body. That means, for example, not yielding to sexual immorality. Your body is not your own, but the Lord's rightful possession, which He purchased with a price. The Holy Spirit resides in your physical body. Instead of abusing, exploiting, and insulting your body by partaking in illicit intercourse or any other practice that defiles our bodies, consecrate it solely for God's purposes and glory. No compromises.

Leviticus 26:11-13; 2 Corinthians 6:16

> *'Are you not of more value than they?'*
> — Matthew 6:26

Look around. See how God provides for lesser creatures than you—birds, plants, fish, animals, and many living things. He cares for them. They have value and are precious in His sight. Yet He has made you alone in His image. You have inherent dignity and greatness. You are more valuable than any other created thing. You are precious to Him.

The point of this inspired question is that Jesus is asking you to trust in God's provision because of how much you matter to Him. You are the height of His creation!

Look in a mirror. Realize that He sees you as His child in Christ. When you see yourself through the lens of the Bible, then you will know how much God cares for and values you, both now and forever. Meditate on this.

Psalm 104:10-18; Luke 12:6-7

'*By what power or by what name did you do this?*'
— Acts 4:7

Some people want to appear superior: to create fear, to manipulate, to embarrass, or to shame other people. Maybe there are similar types of people around you, those who want you embarrassed or shamed because of what you believe. Maybe you know people who want to appear superior to you in order to exalt their own reputation, status, and authority. Or maybe they don't recognize your right as a Christian to practice and proclaim God's word when doing so challenges established precedent, custom, and cultural values.

The good news is that these are God-given opportunities to respond. You can speak the truth in love about Jesus' power and name. Make the most of it. Be prepared. Let them notice the difference in your attitude, actions, and answers. Praise God for such opportunities!

Psalm 146; Matthew 21:23-27

'*Do you now believe?*'
— John 16:31

It might seem ironic that Jesus responds to someone's confession with a question. They confirm that they know and believe in Him. But such a momentary statement in the present—the here and now—doesn't include the future. They still have a long way to go—especially as persecution is about to come their way.

This question applies to you, too. Make sure your confidence is not misplaced. Your confession might have come during an easy time. Make sure when harder times come, you are prepared. Consider your weaknesses now before the trial comes your way.

God will test your faith. Do not be prideful. Do not boast. Do not be confident in yourself. Speak candidly about your weaknesses to God. Prepare yourself for such attacks. Study the Scriptures. Read the stories of the saints. Pursue holiness. Remember the Spirit who is within you.

Proverbs 17:3; Hebrews 12:4-11

> *'And which of you by being anxious can add*
> *a single hour to his span of life?'*
> – Luke 12:25

Worrying is worthless. Being anxious is aimless. You cannot add the smallest amount of time to your life by doing either one. In fact, your life span is out of your control. Rather, every day is a gift of God. Thus, worrying changes nothing.

Recognizing and remembering God is in control, however, changes everything. You no longer have to be anxious about anything. Instead, in everything—with prayer and supplication—make your requests be made known before God. This world is not your home. Trust in God. Walk with Him in peace and righteousness. Focus on Him, not your worries.

Psalm 90:12; Matthew 6:34

> *"Am I not allowed to do what I choose with*
> *what belongs to me?*
> *Or do you begrudge my generosity?"'*
> – Matthew 20:15

God owns everything, and His decisions are perfect. You cannot dispute Him. If He wants to show mercy to one person or group, He is perfectly just in doing it. If He decides to withhold something from you, accept the truth that His decision is perfectly fine, as well. God often recognizes and rewards the good we do, but He is not obligated to do so.

Learn, then, to say and believe, 'Thy will be done.' Avoid talking against others. Assume the roles God has given you. Joyfully serve.

Isaiah 55:8-9; Acts 20:32-36

July

*'And after Paul and Barnabas had no small
dissension and debate with them,
Paul and Barnabas and some of the others were
appointed to go up to Jerusalem to the apostles and
the elders about this question.'*

– Acts 15:2

What causes quarrels and what causes fights among you?
Is it not this, that your passions are at war within you?
— James 4:1

There is a war going on inside of you. Your desires are often envious, prideful, and selfish. From selfish desires come quarrels and fights with others. You lack peace from God because of them. Where there is no divine wisdom or righteousness, there will be power struggles, backstabbing, and conflicts. Whereas we expect to see such attitudes in the world, we need to ensure they do not become ways we treat each other in the church. If your internal desires reflect envy, pride, and selfishness, they will come out externally in your dealings with your Christian brothers and sisters. Conversely, if your inner desires reflect empathy, humility, and selflessness, that will become obvious in your interactions with others. Either way, your actions reveal your heart.

Examine yourself. Humble yourself. Confess your sinful desires. Resist Satan. Draw near to God. In doing so, God will lift you up. Divine wisdom and righteousness will bring peace.

Proverbs 17:14; 1 Peter 2:11-12

'What sort of man is this, that even
winds and sea obey him?'
— Matthew 8:27

You may have encountered some severe storms or other acts of nature, but nothing compares to the supernatural power that Jesus has. Only God can control natural elements such as wind and water. That is why an early follower of Jesus posed this inspired question when he witnessed Jesus quieting a storm. Such a majestic display of power and authority reveals who Jesus is: God in the flesh.

Just imagine! The same Jesus who calmed the storm on the Sea of Galilee is still alive and can do the same thing in your life. He is God. He is present. He is willing to rescue you if you would just look to Him in faith.

Psalm 65:5-8; Mark 4:39

'How can we know the way?'

– John 14:5

If you don't know where you are going, any road will do. But there is only one way to God, and as a believer, you know the way even if you don't understand all the implications of it.

The way to God the Father is only through Christ the Son. But to merely view 'the way' to God in the way you would glance at a road map would be the wrong way to approach Him. The way to God is about your inner commitment to one person, Jesus Christ. It is all about your heart.

Consider whom you really love and why. Look to Jesus. Trust in Him. Commit yourself to Him. Seek Him. If you do, you are on the road to the Father.

Proverbs 12:28; 1 Timothy 2:5-6

Do you not know that if you present yourselves to anyone as obedient slaves, you are slaves of the one whom you obey, either of sin, which leads to death, or of obedience, which leads to righteousness?

– Romans 6:16

The power of sin has been broken in your life because of Jesus Christ. Therefore, you must no longer live as if you are under the power of sin. There is no middle ground. There are no shades of gray when it comes to issues of black and white. You are either a slave of sin or a slave of obedience. You are never free from a master. Unbelievers may think they are free, but they are merely under the illusion created and sustained by Satan.

As a believer, you can enjoy everything without being controlled by anything. Your freedom in Christ is not about doing whatever you want or merely being less obvious in your sinning, but delighting in the freedom you have to obey God willfully, cheerfully, and instinctively. Take pleasure today in the rich and rewarding life you have in Christ.

Proverbs 5:22; John 8:34

'Who then is the faithful and wise manager,
whom his master will set over his household,
to give them their portion of food at the proper time?'

— Luke 12:42

Instead of wondering who is in charge, Jesus wants you to concentrate on what it means to be in charge. You have a responsibility. The Holy Spirit has entrusted you with.gifts to use for the edification of the church. There are consequences to being unprepared, lazy, or negligent. That is why faithfulness is often described in terms of service.

Be faithful. Serve others. God has given you a level of spiritual responsibility over His community. Care for them. God will evaluate you accordingly. Therefore, feed on faithfulness. Befriend faithfulness.

When Jesus returns, will He find you being faithful and busy about God's business, or will He find you unfaithful and at ease, focused on *your* business? Be wise rather than foolish. Be ready all the time. Live out your belief in Jesus. Reflect His love to others. Stay alert.

Genesis 47:11-12; 1 Corinthians 4:1-5

Why then the law?

— Galatians 3:19

A medical examination does not make you sick; it simply reveals your condition. Once properly diagnosed, a doctor may separate you from others until a cure becomes available. In the same way, the law of God did not make people sin; it merely declared existing behaviors to be sins and thus increased people's awareness of them. The law was not the cure, but it provided a type of quarantine until one was made available. The law is good, essential, effective, and God-given. But its role and task are now complete.

The only cure to your sinfulness and the fulfillment of God's promises resides in Jesus Christ. In fact, the problem was never the law but the condition of the people under the law. Inevitably, the law could not control sin. The only answer to the power of sin is in Jesus Christ. He is the remedy. Transfer your trust and allegiance to Jesus. Gladly submit to Him.

Deuteronomy 28:1; Romans 7:12

'Whom do you want me to release for you:
[Jesus] Barabbas, or Jesus who is called Christ?'
– Matthew 27:17

What a stark contrast people were given! Pick your Jesus: the one who strives with a sword to free people (Jesus Barabbas) or the one who sacrifices His life to save sinners (Jesus Christ).

This inspired question, though, still speaks to your current situation. God has given you, too, a similar choice, which is just as stark: the kingdom of God or this world; heaven or hell; the truth or lies; Satan or God. Choose carefully. Don't rush—take time. Test yourself by this question. Make sure that you are able to say honestly that you desire to live for God's glory. Strive to conform your entire life to His.

Isaiah 30:19-22; Matthew 7:13-14

'While it remained unsold, did it not remain your own?
And after it was sold, was it not at your disposal? Why is it
that you have contrived this deed in your heart?'
– Acts 5:4

Our Lord does not require you to sell all your possessions and give them away as a Christian. Everything in the Christian life is voluntary and must come from the heart. At the same time, you cannot lie or seek human praise, especially in the process of giving. It is rebellion against God to do either.

Instead, give liberally, cheerfully, and without show. Support the gospel mission and ministry without the thought of selfish gain, honor, or prestige. Be a good steward of your time, talents, and resources.

Leviticus 10:1-3; Luke 4:12

JULY 9

*'And why do you break the commandment of God
for the sake of your tradition?'*

— Matthew 15:3

You have probably heard someone say, 'But this is how we've always done it.' Indeed, human traditions abound. Ultimate authority, however, must lie with God. Setting aside God's Word for the sake of traditions is a serious offense. It is not that innovation is bad, but fabricated traditions and personal preferences can cause one to go against God's Word. No tradition should overturn Scripture.

Ask yourself on a regular basis whether you draw your teaching and applications from the Scriptures or whether you follow a certain custom because it is traditional. Set aside time each day and each Sabbath to study the Scriptures diligently. Challenge your own understanding of what you do for the sake of tradition. Distinguish between healthy and harmful traditions. Walk by the Word.

Isaiah 29:13-21; Galatians 5:1-15

JULY 10

*Has the potter no right over the clay, to make out of the
same lump one vessel for honorable use and
another for dishonorable use?*

— Romans 9:21

God can use nations or individuals for different purposes according to His sovereign plan of salvation. When trying to explain all this logically, you cannot. What you can do, however, is affirm what the Bible affirms, deny what it denies, and obey what it commands. The sovereignty of God should make believers more humble, reverent, and worshipful—all godly characteristics. Refrain from depriving God of all honor, glory, and majesty due His name. Let this be your only desire—that God may be glorified.

Jeremiah 18:6-10; 2 Timothy 2:20-21

Why are we in danger every hour?
– 1 Corinthians 15:30

Life—especially ministerial life—can be a constant danger. There are dangers of all kinds—both physical and spiritual. The point of recognizing these dangers for what they are is for your protection. You would be foolish to put yourself in a constant state of danger if you had no hope beyond this life. In fact, everything you do as a Christian is absolute nonsense if there is no resurrection. Your struggles and successes are pointless if there is no resurrection.

The good news, however, is that there is a resurrection. You can live without fear because of Christ's resurrection. Let afflictions and troubles find you dead to this world because of it. Endure trials—no matter how hard or how long—in light of it. Think on the centrality of the resurrection in your daily life.

Psalm 142; 2 Corinthians 11:24-28

'Why does this generation seek a sign?'
– Mark 8:12

Sometimes you only see what you want to see. You may be having a hard time discerning God's will—and so you seek a sign; hope for a sign; pray for a sign. You want 100 per cent certainty because it requires no faith, trust, or obedience on your part.

Be careful. Unbelief continually demands authenticating signs. Waiting for a sign out of fear or because of a lack of faith is not good and grieves Jesus. Countless examples already testify to His power and authority. Recall some of them and praise Him. Listen to God assure you, 'I am enough for you!'

Psalm 46; 1 Corinthians 1:22-25

'Did I not tell you that if you believed you would see the glory of God?'

— John 11:40

'Yes!' That is the obvious and only answer. So the answer isn't the problem. Rather, the problem is seeing and discerning God's promise and its significance in relation to Jesus. Jesus then demonstrates His faith and prayer life by thanking God before anything even happens. He prays. He trusts. He knows. There is no doubt in His mind that God will be glorified by this tragic event.

Take a moment to reflect on God's promises to you. Consider Jesus' prayer life and faith. Ask yourself if you are living according to what you say you believe. Do you believe and live what God tells you? Do you have the same confidence and obedience as Jesus? If so, you will likewise see the glory of God in His timing.

Psalm 84:11-12; Philippians 4:19

'"What shall I do, since my master is taking the management away from me?"'

— Luke 16:3

Imagine being fired from your job. You now need to determine what to do and how you can position yourself to find new employment. Instead of moving on too quickly, however, it is best for you to clean up any mess you made. Otherwise, even if you find another job your future will likely be full of pain and regrets, and you'll take a bad reputation with you.

Your window of opportunity is closing fast. As a believer, there are no shortcuts in the Christian life. Take a step forward and work honestly. Be faithful in little as well as in much. Consider your ultimate Boss. Work as if for Him. Glorify Him who gave His all for you. Put into practice the principles Jesus has taught you so plainly in Scripture. Be useful and helpful to others. Desire to walk in newness of life by using your resources to make friends and assist those in need. Do not be dependent upon your surroundings. Depend solely upon Jesus.

Proverbs 6:6-11; Colossians 3:23

Shall we provoke the Lord to jealousy?
Are we stronger than he?
— 1 Corinthians 10:22

The one true God of Christianity will not share His glory with any other so-called god. He alone is worthy of your complete devotion, full worship, and unwavering commitment. Anything else challenges Him, provoking Him to act in judgment. You cannot have any gods in His presence. You cannot eat food consecrated to other so-called deities. Any participation in non-Christian ritual meals is strictly forbidden and is incompatible with your life in Christ.

Do not turn to another religion. Avoid pagan rituals. Embrace and echo the charge of Joshua to Israel: 'As for me and my house, we will serve the Lord.'

Exodus 34:11-16; Revelation 2:14, 20

What do you wish?
Shall I come to you with a rod,
or with love in a spirit of gentleness?
— 1 Corinthians 4:21

God can teach you through a message or through pain. It is your call. Your actions will reveal your choice. If you can listen to the message and apply it to your life, perfect. If you cannot, pain may follow. Allow these inspired questions right now to help you pause and reflect on this contrast. This is not behaviorism, as if God is training a dog. Rather, He is shepherding the hearts of His children. The clear implication is that you must do what the Scripture says as a true believer. But it is your choice whether it will be easy (with love in a spirit of gentleness) or painful (with a rod).

May God give you the grace and courage to apply the message, instead of choosing to experience the pain. If disciplined by God, remember that it is out of His love for you, for your good. Respond with repentance. Recommit yourself today. Place yourself in God's hands.

Proverbs 10:13; Philemon 8-10

JULY 17

'By what authority are you doing these things, and who gave you this authority?'
— Matthew 21:23

Many individuals claim to have authority. But when people do not accept their claims or know the source of their claims, they may challenge those claims. Perhaps people have challenged your authority. Perhaps they look at your credentials to see if they meet their criteria of authority. If they do not, the questioners reject you.

Now think about Jesus. His actions revealed an authority greater than that of some local village preacher from Galilee. The religious leaders, however, knew they had not given Him any such authority and would not accept any claims that it was from God.

Be encouraged. Always return to this basic principle: God grants authority and gives wisdom. Faithfully fulfill the roles God has given you as an ambassador for His Son, and do not get distracted by anyone who rejects or challenges them.

Daniel 2:20-23; John 19:11

JULY 18

'Do you take offense at this?'
— John 6:61

People often do not have a teachable spirit or a willing heart and they are quickly offended when confronted with something new, different, or demanding. Such reactions will necessarily cause divisions. Some will reject such a teaching or worldview. Others will embrace it.

Jesus here is trying to move you past a one-dimensional perception of everything He is saying and doing. There is more than meets the eye. There is another way to interpret His words about physical matters. There is another way of viewing Him—not just as merely a man but also as One who is divine.

Pray, then, for eyes to see and ears to hear Christ's true meaning and purpose. Avoid things that would hamper your progress. Succeed in your duty to study God's Word. Meditate upon Jesus.

Proverbs 22:17-21; Romans 8:7

'What will the owner of the vineyard do?'
– Mark 12:9

This inspired question invites you to be the judge. If you owned an estate, would you continue allowing your tenants to breach your contract with them by not giving you your share of the profits? No, of course not! You just need to remove the current tenants and appoint some new ones. You do not need to destroy the whole estate.

In the same way, God's appointed leaders in Jesus' day were unfaithful and abandoned Him. Therefore, God rejected and replaced them. He removed His presence from among them.

In the twenty-first century, you as a believer are among the new tenants of God's kingdom. Jesus—the chief Cornerstone—is your foundation. Live to serve Him. Seek to understand, represent, and listen to Him at all times. Love Jesus above all else. Give God His due.

Obadiah 21; Romans 11

Am I not free?
Am I not an apostle?
Have I not seen Jesus our Lord?
Are not you my workmanship in the Lord?
– 1 Corinthians 9:1

To get or do whatever you want, you may be tempted to appeal to your 'rights.' Yet knowing your rights is only part of the discussion. There is something far more important than your personal rights—the gospel trumps any rights you may have. Claiming your rights and freedoms over everything else is arrogant and ungodly. Even technically permissible choices might not necessarily be the wisest or most loving courses of action. Sometimes it is best not to act on behalf of your rights and freedoms in Christ. You must be prepared and willing to waive your rights for the sake of the gospel. Know the delights and dangers of your rights and freedoms in Christ. Sacrifice them to serve others. Walk in His ways.

Leviticus 19:9-10; Galatians 5

JULY 21

'Why are you afraid, O you of little faith?'
– Matthew 8:26

You need to see with spiritual eyes, not just physical ones. Seeing a situation as God sees it will quiet your heart in any type of storm. Fearfulness in such situations demonstrates a lack of faith, even though we try to rationalize it or concoct some inner logic. Someone or something has driven God out of your mind and taken His rightful place. This does not mean that dangers in this world are imaginary, but that God is attentive and able to calm any storm.

Thus, change your focus. Even if you only start with a few minutes today, begin shifting your attention from earthly concerns toward heavenly comforts. Keep your heart in continual awe of the majesty of God. Identify the object(s) of your affections. Examine yourself.

A changed heart produces a changed life. Determine often what you are daydreaming about when you are not trying to be holy. Being aware of where your thoughts come from and why will help you gauge and repair your heart.   *Isaiah 41:10; Philippians 4:6-7*

JULY 22

'And if you lend to those from whom you expect to receive, what credit is that to you?'
– Luke 6:34

The focus is not on your money or lending practices but your attitude towards them. You will receive no reward from God if you only give money to people who will pay you back. You need to respond differently from how unbelievers may deal with people. One might expect unbelievers to only make safe loans, protecting themselves as much as possible.

God's people, in contrast, give without strings attached when possible. In fact, the needs of the needy will never get met if people only provide for those who can return the favor. This is not how God or His people operate. Determine what this looks like in your life right now. Write down specific ways. Get started.

Deuteronomy 15:7-11; Matthew 5:42

Who is the liar?

— 1 John 2:22

A core doctrine of the Christian faith is that Jesus Christ is the Messiah, God's promised Deliverer—the One prophesied in the Jewish Scriptures. This belief unites all true believers. Anyone who denies it is a liar. The Bible describes those who reject it as antichrists.

Therefore, you have no relationship with God the Father if you do not know God the Son appropriately. Indeed, you can only know the Father through the Son. Denying the Son's true identity denies the true identity of the Father, who sent the Son and testifies about Him. Do not be deceived, conned, or tricked into believing in some other interpretation of Jesus. Know your Bible. Live in complete and constant submission to God's Word. Listen to solid preaching. Test what you hear with Scripture.

Zechariah 3; John 17:15

You then who teach others, do you not teach yourself?
While you preach against stealing, do you steal?
You who say that one must not commit adultery,
do you commit adultery?
You who abhor idols, do you rob temples?

— Romans 2:21-22

Knowing and doing are two different things. You may know you are thirsty, but that alone will not quench your thirst. You must drink. You may know you are hungry—but that alone will not nourish your body. You must eat. You may know the truth of God's Word—but that alone will not help you. You must apply it. It does not matter how much knowledge you have, what gifts you possess, or anything else you believe about yourself if your claims and your conduct do not go hand-in-hand.

Take time now to examine yourself. Avoid or correct inappropriate behavior. Become a godly Christian. Emerge victorious.

Ezekiel 33:30-32; Titus 1:16

JULY 25

'Lord, do you want us to tell fire to come down
from heaven and consume them?'
— Luke 9:54

Your special relationship with God should never be used for self-interest. When your self-centered desire to call upon divine authority to mercilessly and maliciously punish even legitimate wrongs is greater than your love and compassion toward people, it deserves a rebuke. At least that is what Jesus does here to two of His disciples, James and John (*aka* 'Sons of Thunder'), when some people He was going to visit did not receive Him warmly. Vengeance is God's—not ours.

Retaliation has no place in the kingdom of God. At most, cut ties and move on. Leave immoral things for immoral people. Fulfill the things God has commanded you. Live in harmony with others. Intercede for others. Testify to Christ—warning, persuading, and calling others. Show acts of love.

2 Kings 1:9-18; 2 Peter 3:8-9

JULY 26

'For what will it profit a man if he gains the whole
world and forfeits his soul?'
— Matthew 16:26

If you never come to know Christ, your life will lead to eternal punishment. No amount of earthly accomplishments will change this fact.

Think about it. You could succeed at everything you do, but still fail in life because you succeeded at all the wrong things. Nothing you do apart from Christ will benefit you in the end. Nothing in this world compares to the immeasurable value of your soul.

Knowing you are capable of such great self-destruction, you must deny yourself. You cannot expect spiritual health if you are constantly gratifying the flesh and every impulse. Regulate your life so that you will not be influenced in your decisions by worldly concerns. Consider that the good of your soul is of utmost importance. Thank God for granting you life until now.

Ezekiel 18:4; Romans 6:23

'Do you want to be healed?'
– John 5:6

Jesus takes the initiative to heal, both then and now. He looks for people in need. But this inspired question tells you much more about His intentions than His initiative. He doesn't ask for medical details or the physical symptoms you are experiencing. Jesus simply wants to know if you really want to be completely healed, for only Jesus can fully cure you. Only He can give you new life here and everlasting life after this one.

No doctor, medicine, or bandage can cure your deepest ills. You need spiritual cleansing. Yes, physical healing is great and may come, but even more miraculous and important is the spiritual healing that occurs when your sins are forgiven and you are spared an eternity in Hell.

Be healed. Believe in Jesus. Remember that faith is an activity, something you have to apply to your life. Regard your current circumstances and conditions as part of God's work of perfecting you. Whether the trial is permanent or passing, do exactly what Jesus tells you.

Psalm 147:3; 1 Peter 2:24

'What is your decision?'
– Mark 14:64

As always, you have a choice to make. You can believe the lies, false witnesses, and lack of evidence. Or you can trust Jesus' words, deeds, and miracles. When a governor weighed a decision about Jesus' fate, the chief priests, elders, and scribes unanimously decided to put Jesus to death. They condemned Him on the charge of blasphemy. Yet Jesus—although in full control—did not resist or condemn them in return. He demonstrated that He was the promised Messiah by suffering as a servant.

This is a model for all Christians, including you. The path to glory involves suffering. False accusations might be levied against you. Someone might falsely accuse you. But will you take up your cross like Jesus? Will you suffer injustice for a righteous case? What is your decision?

Psalm 119:71; 1 Peter 5:10

'Men, why are you doing these things?'
— Acts 14:15

Sometimes you cannot start with the gospel. You first need to address someone's behavior. You lovingly need to tell them they are heading down the wrong road. You may even need to go further back into the story of God's redeeming work in order to bring some people you meet up to speed on God's saving work in Jesus Christ. Otherwise, they may remain in their obstinateness and absolute denial of Jesus.

Time is short. Help them to be wise. Stand in the gap. Lead them to Christ. Take time now to pray for them!

Malachi 1:6-14; Luke 1:16-17

JULY 30

'"Did you not agree with me for a denarius?"'
— Matthew 20:13

The voice of the Holy Spirit will never prompt you to say or think, 'I want my fair share; I'm entitled to it; God owes me!' You may not understand why someone else receives a blessing, but the kingdom of heaven is about more than just contractual obligations. We cannot calculate the measure or distribution of God's goodness and grace.

If you become jealous, you are in danger. You may become like the brother in Jesus' Prodigal Son parable, who did nothing wrong, but became full of envy when his brother, destitute due to his own foolishness, came humbly home to a lavish, forgiving fatherly welcome.

Be encouraged by God's generosity. Extend the same. Rejoice rather than complain when someone else receives grace. Act with integrity. Respond with love.

Deuteronomy 15:7-11; 1 Timothy 6:17-19

> *'What is this conversation that you are holding*
> *with each other as you walk?'*
> – Luke 24:17

People can be disappointed by a sad and seemingly hopeless event, and even talk about it with others at length, without realizing God's presence among them. They completely miss the spiritual aspect—and thus, they remain in their sad and depressed state.

May that never happen to you! Challenge yourself. Believe God's Word is true. Do not trust your heart and mind alone. Receive God's Word with your mind and the Holy Spirit will enable the truth to become clear to your spirit. Take such sad and depressing times in your life as wonderful opportunities to prove your faith, show your faith, manifest your faith, and bring glory to God.

Jeremiah 13:15-17; John 16:20-22

August

*'Being at a loss how to investigate these questions,
I asked whether he wanted to go to Jerusalem and
be tried there regarding them.'*

– Acts 25:20

'Simon, are you asleep? Could you not watch one hour?'
– Mark 14:37

One day, you proclaim your unfailing loyalty. But the very next day, you cannot even stay awake for one hour praying. The problem is not whether you have enough discipline or time. You can easily think of instances when you stayed out all night partying, waited in line for hours just to buy something, watched television all day, cheered on a sports team in a stadium for hours, or camped out to buy tickets to something.

The reality is that you need a deeper commitment to spiritual things, with no compromise. Otherwise, when temptations come, they will overwhelm you and you will fall away. Discipline yourself at all times. Convert wasted time into time spent with God. Always remember: Mediocrity is for those who serve lesser gods, not yours.

Proverbs 3:3; Matthew 6:9-13

'Who is the greatest in the kingdom of heaven?'
– Matthew 18:1

Everyone wants to be the best, in the top position above everyone else. According to God's value scale, however, it is not the greatest who will be first. Just as children are dependent on their parents or guardians, so will the greatest of God's children be dependent on Him. God exalts the humble. Status, therefore, in the kingdom of heaven, is reversed. Humble believers will be the greatest in the kingdom of heaven.

Always strive for humility. Beware of spiritual pride. Prioritize others over yourself. Beg the Lord to use you greatly in His service.

Proverbs 22:4; Philippians 2:3-11

Who is to condemn?
– Romans 8:34

Fear not. Your boss, your job, the people around you, and even the government may hurt you. But none of them will ever triumph over you. No one stands to condemn you because Jesus intercedes on your behalf in the presence of God the Father. No matter what charges or accusations the world or Satan throw at you, they amount to nothing before the Lord. He declares you righteous in Christ, and therefore, there is no condemnation. By grace through faith, His blood covers your sins—past, present, and future. You are clothed in His righteousness. Now walk in a manner worthy of this truth. Do everything unto the glory of God.

Psalm 34:22; Hebrews 7:24-25

'Nevertheless, when the Son of Man comes, will he find faith on earth?'
– Luke 18:8

Understand that your faith is going to be tried. Storms and trials will come. But thank God you are in His hands.

So submit yourself to Him. Be content to be in His grip. Maintain your faith and prayer life until Jesus returns. Do not keep your eye on the clock, but keep it on Him and His work. Persist in living out your faith. Be ready and waiting. Keep your mind prepared and ready to obey promptly by knowing, believing, and obeying God's Word.

Psalm 46; Hebrews 10:23-26

For am I now seeking the approval of man, or of God?
Or am I trying to please man?

– Galatians 1:10

Do not be a 'people pleaser'—living for their acceptance. It is incompatible with following Jesus. This does not mean do the opposite and irritate people. The point is that you should seek God's approval first. You only have one Lord and Master. Your total focus should be to please Him. And if anyone accuses you—as they did the Apostle Paul—of being a people pleaser, provide examples of how you are not, just as Paul did.

Focus on pleasing God. Examine yourself today. Embrace the mission that God has given you—to glorify and serve Him and to make disciples for Him. Make sure you are pleasing Him.

1 Samuel 16:7; 1 Thessalonians 2:3-8

'What are you arguing about with them?'

– Mark 9:16

Right after having one of the greatest mountaintop experiences of all time (encountering the presence and majesty of God by way of the Transfiguration), the disciples failed miserably in ministry. At the heart of their failure was unbelief. It does not really matter who was arguing.

The point of this inspired question is to find the underlying cause of the problem: the illness of a boy. Jesus goes on to criticize the entire generation because unbelief is representative of it. Sadly, not even the disciples had the faith and prayer to deliver the boy from demonic possession.

Thankfully, Jesus defeats the demons, and therefore, the illness. What a great lesson in surrendering to Jesus and the power of prayer. Remember that unbelief and lack of prayer are dangerous. You cannot succeed on your own. You are dependent on God. Trust in Him. Devote yourself to prayer. God's help and power are available to you if you will just look to Him and obey Him in faith.

Deuteronomy 20:2-4; Jude 9

AUGUST 7

'Why do you not understand what I say?'

— John 8:43

Your actions reveal your heart. The point of Jesus' inspired question here is to get you thinking about whether you are hearing, understanding, and obeying God's voice. If you have already made up your mind about someone or something, you will not be able to hear and obey what that person has commanded. Even if you know better, you will be incapable of accepting and applying the truth—for true knowledge is impossible apart from God.

To know God is to know what He says, commands, and teaches. The more you understand God's Word, the more you will trust, love, and obey Him. Go to God. Confess any shortcomings. Have His Word at your instant and constant disposal. Learn how to listen to His voice and hear the truth about yourself. Remember that it is a sin to doubt God's Word. Ask for spiritual discernment and understanding. Always do as He leads you.

Jeremiah 6:10; Luke 8:11-15

AUGUST 8

'For which is easier, to say, "Your sins are forgiven," or to say, "Rise and walk"?'

— Matthew 9:5

People make claims all the time. Some claims are true; others are false. The easiest claims to make are those that are virtually impossible to either prove or disprove, thereby preventing people from disproving the claim.

Jesus had commanded a disabled man to walk, and the man had done so. But the man's new ability to walk provided visible evidence that Jesus' ability to forgive sins is real. You can quickly understand that it is one thing to declare someone forgiven of their sins since no one can test or disprove the claim, but it is quite another thing to fully restore a paralyzed person, since everyone can see the evidence in front of them.

Jesus uses this logic to His advantage. Tangible evidence that Jesus can supernaturally heal confirms His authority to forgive you of your sins. Become convinced in your heart that there is no limit to Jesus' power and authority. Your anxiety and unsettledness will end when you fully trust in Him.

Jeremiah 32:26-27; Luke 1:37

'How is it that you have agreed together to test the Spirit of the Lord?'
– Acts 5:9

Deceiving the people of God is a direct challenge to God. It is an act of pride, as well as greed. God will hold you accountable for all your actions, even if you were merely an accomplice. There is no hiding or faking the truth. God is all-knowing. He knows your motives.

Turn away from this type of self-destruction. Say no to conspiracies. Replace rebellion with submission. Trust in His provisions. Walk in the Spirit. Make no provision for the flesh.

Deuteronomy 6:16-17; Matthew 4:7

'Why was the ointment wasted like that?'
– Mark 14:4

You may get angry when it appears that someone has wasted a valuable resource. But you may also lack the spiritual insight regarding what it is being used for, as Judas did here.

Nothing is ever wasted if it is devoted to Jesus. He deserves your best. No sacrifice—not even death—is too much to ask of you. In fact, sacrificial love is at the core of what it means to be a true disciple. Look at Jesus. His sacrifice was most precious of all—and yet it was anything but wasted.

He sacrificed everything for you. Follow Him and offer your best. Be willing, like the Apostle Paul, to pour yourself out like an offering given completely in the service of God. Give willingly, cheerfully, and without show. Use earthly things for your spiritual advancement. Set your affections on things above.

2 Kings 9:1-3; 2 Corinthians 9:7

If all were a single member, where would the body be?

— 1 Corinthians 12:19

By divine appointment, every follower of Jesus has a distinct place in the body of Christ. We are not all the same (praise God!). But we do all need each other to maximize our efficiency. All our diversity must function in unity.

No matter what anyone thinks, we all need each other to function properly. For the world to see a portrait—not a caricature—of the body of Christ, we need unity in diversity. Recognize that each of us are made in the image of God, and remember that God has called us to a life of being of benefit to others. If you exhibit this kind of attitude and love, you will glorify God and enrich the lives of others.

Judges 20:8-11; Ephesians 4:11-16

'What shall I do, Lord?'

— Acts 22:10

If you plan to live tomorrow, ask this question. If you want success, happiness, or contentment, ask this question. In fact, ask this question every day because of Jesus' presence in your life. Whether He tells you to go here or there, seek the risen Lord to direct you. Turn to the Lord in faith, and pursue His guidance wholeheartedly. Listen and heed His voice. Be ready to do whatever He says. Oh, what an important question to ask regularly!

Psalm 32:8; James 4:10

'Is it I, Rabbi?'
– Matthew 26:25

You might not think Jesus knows about something you did, or at least you hope He doesn't. Maybe you covered it up well. Maybe He has already forgotten about it, you tell yourself. Maybe God is not ever-present and all-knowing, you imagine.

The truth of the matter, however, is that all those attempts to reason sin away are wrong. It is impossible to hide from God. Everything is laid bare before Him, even the intentions of your heart.

You cannot hide from God. That has been humanity's inclination since the Fall of Adam. Instead, return to God. Realize the truth about yourself. Cast your burdens on Him. Resolve to amend your life with the help of God's grace. Celebrate the rest He provides in Christ, and strive to enter that rest.

Psalm 41:8-10; Hebrews 4:12-13

'Do you say this of your own accord, or did others say it to you about me?'
– John 18:34

Jesus asks Pilate if he is really interested in knowing whether Jesus is the King of the Jews, or whether he is just interrogating Jesus because of what he heard from others in his role as Roman governor. Although Pilate does not answer Jesus' question here, it is a great question for you to consider. Jesus wants to know your motivations, too. Your curiosity and understanding of His true identity ought to come from within yourself, rather than only from others. When you seek answers of your own accord, Jesus is ready to answer them or clarify any concerns. He does not, however, accommodate indifference.

Therefore, always gauge your heart. Remind yourself that the Scriptures make it plain and clear that God weighs your motives. Take your sincere questions, doubts, fears, and concerns to Him. In confidence, make your requests known to Him. He delights in blessing you. He is always concerned about your welfare. He has purchased your ultimate good in Jesus Christ.

Proverbs 21:2; Matthew 6:1

'What were you discussing on the way?'
– Mark 9:33

Sometimes, a person does not really ask questions such as this to gain information; and certainly Jesus already knew the answer. Still, this kind of question is a good way to get someone else to realize and vocalize his or her foolishness.

After reading the Bible or hearing a sermon, you may start thinking more highly of yourself than you ought. You may even quote verses verbatim or debate with someone else about who is more important. In moments like that, do not forget this inspired question, and remember that Jesus knows your thoughts and conversations. As Jesus' disciple, avoid all prideful conversations. Challenge your thoughts. Sacrificially serve and do not vie for the highest place of honor. Seek to be a servant. Leave your greatness and exaltation up to God. For God exalts the humble.

Proverbs 29:23; Matthew 23:12

Who serves as a soldier at his own expense?
Who plants a vineyard without eating any of its fruit?
Or who tends a flock without getting some of the milk?
– 1 Corinthians 9:7

The answers to these inspired questions should be obvious: no one, no one, and no one. Everyone gets their fair share. Every soldier is paid; every vinedresser eats grapes; every shepherd drinks milk. You, too, in your everyday life are sustained by your labor. You do something and receive something. So it is with ministers of the gospel. They should expect to be supported by those under their care. Their work is great and worthy of your financial support. Let those elders who labor well in preaching and teaching be considered worthy of double honor. Make a commitment. Give regularly.

Proverbs 27:18; 1 Timothy 5:17-18

'What do you want me to do for you?'
— Matthew 20:32

This inspired question is for all believers, including you. What do you want Jesus to do for you? Similarly, Jesus' response is a model for all believers, including you. He stops to address the needs of people who are down and out. Even when facing something catastrophic, He pauses to care for others in the midst of what might seem to be a hopeless situation.

If you only had a few days to live, would you spend time helping beggars on the side of the street? Jesus did. At the very least, ask God how you may serve others today, this week, and this year. Look for ways to serve. Minister to the needs of others. Volunteer your time and talents, even when it is inconvenient for you to do so.

Isaiah 42:5-9; Luke 4:16-20

*'But if you do not believe his writings,
how will you believe my words?'*
— John 5:47

You have the right Scriptures, but Jesus asks if you really believe them. The Scriptures and Jesus stand or fall together. Your salvation depends on Jesus and His Word. Jesus here accuses these religious leaders of not really believing the Scriptures, though they have devoted their lives to reading and studying. They might be immersed in analyzing them and able to quote from them, but there is much more to God's Word than just words. Learn this great and vital lesson.

Take this inspired question seriously. Be sure you really believe the Scriptures—all of them. Read all the Scriptures in light of Jesus. Pray for God to open the eyes of your heart. Obey with your whole heart.

Amos 2:4-5; Acts 15:21

> *"'What shall I do, for I have nowhere*
> *to store my crops?'"*
> – Luke 12:17

Did you notice how utterly self-absorbed this person is? Yes, he refers to himself three times in just this one question. 'Me, myself, and I!' That is often the focus of someone who—having earned great wealth—has learned to trust in himself. The person has created his or her own private kingdom. Satan has kept such a self-centered person in the bliss of life; unrepentant. One major problem with this scenario is that this person seeks satisfaction where none can be found: this world.

There is nothing wrong with earning wealth. But no matter how successful you are financially, you cannot acquire or store enough material possessions to satisfy your spiritual needs. Not only will you grow weary and remain dissatisfied, you will never be content. What a loss that would be! Such a state is similar to that of a gluttonous person who—though having access to the most wonderful foods—quickly gobbles it down without sharing or even enjoying it, being so preoccupied with thinking about what else remains to be devoured.

Consider this carefully. Living rich and dying cursed is not a great plan for your life. Flee these things. Concentrate on the things that will remain forever. Choose to have less rather than more. Say no to something you want every day, for doing so will help you stay in the practice of wanting less. Go and visit those less fortunate than you. Your visits will not only stir up compassion and thankfulness inside of you, but they will help you guard against being discontented.

Proverbs 30:7-9; 1 Timothy 6:17

Who are you to pass judgment on
the servant of another?

– Romans 14:4

Whether you are rich or poor, mature or immature, well-educated or untrained, you do not have the right to judge a fellow believer in non--essential issues. In matters that do not pertain to right beliefs or godly behavior, accept every other believer. Everyone will stand or fall based on God's judgment, not yours. You are not better. You are not their ultimate judge. You are not God. Therefore, do not respond according to your sinful nature.

Living in Christ is not about being right or wrong on issues of diet, dress, or such things (so long as they are within godly parameters). It is about being rightly related with God and others. You must continually guard yourself from yourself. Let this inspired question be a warning to you to keep yourself humble. Let go of your selfish requirements and petty preferences. Instead, focus on partaking of the bread of life and on clothing yourself with Christ.

Psalm 75:6-7; James 4:12

For who sees anything different in you?
What do you have that you did not receive?
If then you received it,
why do you boast as if you did not receive it?
– 1 Corinthians 4:7

It should be evident to everyone who sees you that you live a radically different life than any nonbeliever. Of course, the reason you are profoundly different is not because of you, but Christ who lives in you. Thus, remain humble all the days of your life. Do not under-or over-estimate who you are or what you are capable of. Rather, be thankful for the gifts and talents God has given you. Develop a grateful spirit. Be totally honest with yourself. Stay focused on God so that you will constantly acknowledge that everything—absolutely everything—you have has been given to you as a gift. All is of grace. Everything is a gift. Nothing is deserved.

Keep these inspired questions in your mind to help you see the foolishness of any type of boasting except in the cross of your Lord Jesus Christ.

Jeremiah 9:23; 2 Corinthians 11:30

'Where are we to get enough bread in such a
desolate place to feed so great a crowd?'
– Matthew 15:33

Perhaps your circumstances look bad. You presume you are in a helpless predicament. Your physical resources are limited or inadequate. You feel things are simply too much for you to handle. You don't immediately recall the last time Jesus performed a miracle in your life. You feel utterly helpless.

Be encouraged. God is still sovereign, merciful, and benevolent. Know that His help is available. Consider how many provisions God has already provided you. Let each provision you receive be a reminder and a guide to His loving care for you now and always. Rest in God's love.

Psalm 136; John 21:4-6

'Who made you a ruler and a judge over us?'
– Acts 7:27

Some questions arise from people who do not see God's handiwork. They are quick to point out that you are no better than they are. They may even double down and put up a wall. Granted, we are not called to judge unbelievers. God alone elects. God alone separates the wheat from the chaff. God alone is the final judge. But if people foolishly reject you or your God-given message, they are rejecting Christ.

When tempted by Satan or when accused by others, seek out God's presence. Recognize your own weaknesses so that you will rely on God's grace, which is sufficient for you.

Genesis 45:24; Luke 12:42

'Can anything good come out of Nazareth?'
– John 1:46

Stereotypes. Rivalries. Skepticism. All of these can hinder your witness and distract you from the truth. Even more, the same blinding power of these issues can come when you are sharing about Jesus with someone. In this discussion among the disciples, what one person (Philip) accepted, another person (Nathanael) did not. Nathanael could not imagine anything good coming out of a place he distrusted. Perhaps you have heard or asked a similar question about a person from a community that has a bad reputation—a ghetto, a barrio, a slum, or a similar place—'How can a person from there be a force for good?'

After you encounter Jesus, those types of thoughts must go away. You put away your ungodly prejudices, examine the truth for yourself, and form an opinion based on personal experience. Make it your aim to guard your mind against preconceived notions of people, places, and ideas. Pray to be delivered from them. Seek righteousness. Follow Jesus.

Proverbs 24:23; Acts 10:34-43

Are not those who eat the sacrifices participants in the altar?
— 1 Corinthians 10:18

As a believer, you have a testimony and relationship with Jesus that should supersede any right or freedom you may have. This needs to be expressed in real-life situations. One such setting and opportunity for you to demonstrate your priorities is at mealtime. Formally or informally, you cannot partake in ceremonial meals of other religions because it is considered as being idolatry. If you join in, you are necessarily identifying with the false religion. This is incompatible with the gospel. Gain a more objective understanding. God's eyes are always upon you. Hate what God hates. Love what God loves. Honor Him in all things.

Daniel 1:8; Acts 15:28-29

'*When therefore the owner of the vineyard comes, what will he do to those tenants?*'
— Matthew 21:40

Anyone with a sense of justice who reads this inspired question in Jesus' parable of the murderous tenants who kill a vineyard owner's son will recognize the only reasonable answer. The owner will not merely evict the tenants—he will destroy them. He will inflict capital punishment upon them for murdering his son. The punishment fits the crime. Justice will be done.

The same principle applies to you. If you—being under the supreme authority of God the Father—reject Jesus, you will come to a miserable eternal end, for God is just. But if you accept Jesus, you will find rest. Follow Jesus, and He will lead you to true holiness and happiness.

2 Chronicles 24:20-22; Acts 7:51-53

'Where did this man get these things?
What is the wisdom given to him?
How are such mighty works done by his hands?'
— Mark 6:2

Even when you do not get to hear a teaching or witness an action directly, the responses of people can clue you in to what is happening. Here, the words and deeds of Jesus are shocking people. Yet their astonishment leads to their rejection of Jesus. They are offended by His teaching, which lacks any clear conventional source, such as a rabbi or formal schooling. He does not fit neatly into their previously established mental box.

A similar principle may be true in your life. The hardest people for you to reach may be those closest to you. Family, friends, and neighbors may reject your words and deeds, even if the words and deeds are correct and godly, simply because they are beyond their comprehension (because spiritual things are spiritually discerned). Nevertheless, stay the course. Be faithful to your calling. Expound and explain the truth of God to those who cannot understand it in the hope that God may perhaps grant them repentance leading to a knowledge of the truth.

Ezekiel 2:1-7; Acts 14:19-23

What then? Are we Jews any better off?
— Romans 3:9

In one sense, Jews are no better off than anyone else is in this world. They—like you—are condemned under sin unless they turn to Jesus Christ by faith. God makes no exceptions. No one is righteous apart from Christ. Everyone is in desperate need of the gospel—not just because they sinned, but also because they are enslaved to sin apart from Christ. What God does through Christ is this: He breaks the stronghold of sin restraining your life and sets you free.

Be thankful for God's grace. Lift up your heart, mind, and voice to worship Him today.

Ecclesiastes 7:20; Galatians 3:15-29

> *'What did you go out into the wilderness to see?*
> *A reed shaken by the wind?'*
> — Luke 7:24

People do not always travel just to admire the scenery of a place. Sometimes, they have ulterior motives. Here, Jesus highlights the fact that some people did not just journey out to the wilderness to see the landscape. They went for other reasons: to see a spectacle; to witness a person; to hear a prophecy. But regardless of the reason, Jesus wants to get to the heart of the matter.

This question offers an opportunity to gauge why you are drawn to certain places and events. What are your motives? What do you expect to see? What is your understanding of the situation? Are you there for godly reasons? Are you open to what God is doing?

1 Chronicles 19:1-5; John 1:19-25

> *'Simon, son of John, do you love me more than these?'*
> — John 21:15

Every time Jesus asks someone if they love Him, He gives them a directive. What is more, in this case He doesn't just ask whether Simon loves Him, but whether he loves Him 'more than these.' He is testing Simon. It doesn't matter what 'these' refers to—the fish; his nets; the fishing boat and gear; other people. Or, most likely, 'these' refers to the other disciples nearby listening to the exchange. Whatever or whoever it is, nothing and no one compares to Jesus.

In the same way, He deserves your utmost affections. He expects your highest obedience. Recall and respond to these precious words of your sweet Savior: 'If you love me, you will keep my commandments . . . If you keep my commandments, you will abide in my love.' Recite them often. Never waste your time in the present. Live only to please Him.

Deuteronomy 11:13-15; 2 John 6

'What do I still lack?'
— Matthew 19:20

You have led a relatively good life as far as you can tell, but there still seems to be something missing. There is a longing inside of you that has not yet been satisfied. As you reflect on the future and on taking hold of the eternal life to which you were called, you want to know if you lack anything. Are you missing the mark or falling short of God's standard?

The answer to your uncertainty is easy, but the path to eternal life is narrow. You must submit to God's will and follow Jesus in a life of discipleship. Rest assured, there is nothing pertaining to your salvation that Jesus keeps secret. There is no hidden agenda. There is no riddle you must solve. Rather, you must cling to Jesus and follow Him.

Cast away your idols. Do not put off doing so. Decide right now with the help of God's grace to amend your life going forward. Pursue conformity to Christ.

Joshua 22:29; John 10:1-5

September

'The high priest then questioned Jesus about his disciples and his teaching.'

– John 18:19

'Where is the promise of his coming?'

– 2 Peter 3:4

Unbelievers have always mocked Christians for what they believe, especially in relation to the return of Christ. It seems comical to them that you believe there is a divine judgment coming.

On the one hand, your belief that Jesus will return soon seems justifiable. Jesus first promised His return thousands of years ago, and Christ followers were already asking about Christ's delay in the first century after His resurrection. On the other hand, God's promises have never been wrong—and His prophecies have never gone unfulfilled. You know God will indeed judge the whole world, and He will do it according to His predetermined plan. We do not know when, but we know it will happen.

Until Jesus does return, capitalize on His delay. Be fruitful. Fulfill your calling. Proclaim the gospel. There is still much work to be done. The promise of His coming, though it has not happened yet, is as sure as His resurrection. And His resurrection is as sure as the coming final judgment. Be prepared.

Amos 9:11-15; Matthew 24:36-44

'Rabbi, who sinned, this man or his parents, that he was born blind?'

– John 9:2

'Your sin or lack of faith is why bad things happen to you.' This is what some people believe. They assume that only good things happen to good people and bad things happen to bad people. Such was the theology of Job's friends in the Old Testament. Instead of comforting him, they accused him—as if to say, 'You are to blame for everything bad in your life.'

Instead of focusing on the cause of the problem here, however, Jesus wants you to center your attention on God's purpose for it. Discover how God can use your problem(s) right now to demonstrate His power. Realize that God uses various methods in the process of your spiritual growth. Find ways to bring Him glory through your current hardships. Identify God's hand in your life despite your circumstances and then praise Him.

Exodus 4:11; Luke 22:42

> *'Teacher, what good deed must I*
> *do to have eternal life?'*
> — Matthew 19:16

Notice that this inspired question assumes the answer is that you can do something to earn your salvation. Now consider ways people today may suppose they have earned it: performing good deeds, saying a prayer, filling out a card, walking down an aisle, partaking in the sacraments, knowing the Bible, taking a class, speaking in tongues, and on and on. All of these actions, however, would be salvation by good works.

Yet that is not the good news of the gospel of Jesus Christ. In that way of thinking, salvation becomes an economy where the currency is deeds—ones which, in the end, somehow add up to the purchase of a priceless gift. Surprisingly, though, Jesus does reply with something to do. His point, however, is not that you can inherit the kingdom of heaven by your own merits. Rather, you will have eternal life if you follow the path of discipleship, which requires you to embrace Jesus and obediently follow Him in faith. The gospel message calls for you to repent and turn to God, performing deeds in keeping with your repentance. But the spiritual life to which God calls us is something we are incapable of doing on our own. Thankfully, God—in His infinite mercy—has addressed your inadequacies in the gospel of Jesus Christ.

Go to Jesus. Love God the Father through God the Son by means of God the Holy Spirit above all else.

Genesis 15:6; Ephesians 2:8-10

'"What is this that I hear about you?"'
– Luke 16:2

What others say about you is sometimes true. It is not always just gossip or rumor. The context of this inspired question concerns employment. Imagine poorly handling the financial affairs of a rich person or a company. Your boss would not keep silent about it, because not pointing out your failure would lead to more harm. You have left your supervisor with only one decision—to let you go.

Yet even in the midst of losing your job or experiencing another misfortune that might affect your livelihood, damage your reputation, or hinder your future, you can use your time wisely. For instance, you can try to make things right. In fact, that is something that you—yourself—have to do, if able to. Put things right. You have to do that: you, yourself. Assess your situation. Come up with a strategy. Seek forgiveness. Plead with God to give you clear insight. Make a decision to do right. Use what has been entrusted to you.

Wealth will not last, but people will. Take the time and effort to build new and better relationships. Make friends. Reap eternal rewards.

1 Samuel 2:22-26; Revelation 20:12

'For what should I ask?'

– Mark 6:24

A younger generation often looks to an older one for guidance. This inspired question appears within an account of a wicked king who has promised his young stepdaughter anything she wants. She does not know what to ask for, so she asks her mother what to request. Sadly, the mother's wickedness and pursuit of revenge get passed down to and through her daughter. What is worse, the person in leadership complies with her evil request because of social pressure. He authorizes the murder of a godly man, John the Baptist.

Many lessons can be drawn from this inspired story, but the main point is that proclaiming the gospel—to people either young or old—will often be met with hostility and even death. John the Baptist fulfilled the ministry God had called him to, even to the point of being beheaded.

Keep the faithfulness to your calling in mind as you live for Jesus, go on mission, and pray for missionaries. Everyone dies. Everyone's life disappears like a vapor. Make sure your priorities are correct. Be an ambassador for Christ to people both young and old. Set your affections on things above.

1 Kings 21:1-16; Revelation 20:4-6

'What do you think? If a man has a hundred sheep, and one of them has gone astray, does he not leave the ninety-nine on the mountains and go in search of the one that went astray?'

– Matthew 18:12

The picture here is of an insider who has strayed and is being led back into the fold, not of an outsider being brought into the fold. You—like God—should pursue straying believers. You should care for them like God cares. No matter what member might be in spiritual danger, you should take action to get them back and to protect them.

By doing so, you shepherd like the one true Shepherd. Strive to bring back those who wander. Believe that God can use you. Consider how to help others. Have a plan. Rise up and assume responsibility.

Ezekiel 34:1-24; James 5:19-20

'Do you understand what you are reading?'
— Acts 8:30

You probably have more opportunities to proclaim Jesus than you realize. There is no need to be intimidated, shy, or pessimistic about it. Pray for open doors and the ability to recognize them. Obey the Spirit's prompting and work. In doing so, you will be fulfilling the Great Commission. Immerse yourself in God's glorious service. Labor for souls.

God has entrusted you with His truth. Do not forget or neglect your duty. Be wise. Be bold. Be proactive. Initiate spiritual conversations. Go now.

Nehemiah 8:1-8; Luke 24:25-27

Are not the rich the ones who oppress you, and the ones who drag you into court?
— James 2:6

Many people idolize the rich. Yet ironically, it is rich people who will often haul you into court. Once you do not meet their demands, they throw a tantrum. They take advantage of you financially. They oppress the poor. They even exploit the justice system to get their way, especially since they have additional connections, deep pockets, and a bent for exercising their power and influence over people.

Despite those realities, we know that there is a God who is in absolute control, owns everything, and cannot be bribed. And yet those rich people—who have so many physical blessings to thank God for—may blaspheme His name.

Remember often this inspired question, then. Social ranking is for unbelievers, not Christians. Let Christ's love for you be the model for your love toward others.

Amos 4:1; Matthew 6:24

> *Are all apostles? Are all prophets? Are all teachers?*
> *Do all work miracles?*
> *Do all possess gifts of healing? Do all speak with tongues?*
> *Do all interpret?*
> — 1 Corinthians 12:29-30

The intended answer to all seven inspired questions is, 'Of course not!' Every believer has at least one gift. No one has them all. The gift or gifts a believer has should be used to benefit the body of Christ.

Focus on the unifying purpose and power of these diverse gifts so that the whole body will function properly and with maximum efficiency. Stay involved in your community. Seek to serve one another. Hear the insights of others. Make decisions for the benefit of the whole body of Christ.

Jeremiah 13:11; 1 Peter 4:10-11

> *'Is a lamp brought in to be put under a basket,*
> *or under a bed, and not on a stand?*
> — Mark 4:21

The secret of God's kingdom is widely available and not hidden. Just as a lamp's purpose is to light up a room, so Jesus' purpose for His divine revelation is for it to shine forth and light up the world.

If you ask, the Holy Spirit will open your mind and heart to see and act upon the truths of the parables. The truths are often the opposite of what you might expect. The kingdom of God is not about a great monarch coming to rule over His people—it's about a lowly, suffering servant whom you must listen to, believe in, and actively follow.

Merely hearing, knowing, and obeying some commandments is inadequate. Respond to Jesus' call. Follow and obey Him. God demands nothing less than your total allegiance. Do not think for one minute that after you become a Christian you can just go through the motions. Live and function as a child of light.

Psalm 119:105; Matthew 5:14-16

*'Do you think that these Galileans were worse
sinners than all the other Galileans, because
they suffered in this way?'*
– Luke 13:2

Jesus wants you to identify and consider the spiritual implications of tragic events going on around you rather than focusing on political decisions
that may have caused these events. Jesus wants you to, indeed, be aware
that bad things did and still do happen to people. But He wants you to
understand that such horrific tragedies are not necessarily due to them
being any worse sinners than you. Real and present dangers are at everyone's front door. Your life is just as fragile as another person's. Disaster
looms for you just like it did or does for them.

Thus, in the aftermath of a deadly disaster, consider what is going to
happen to you when you die. You must repent just like everyone else if
you are going to be saved from God's eternal judgment and torture. Get a
clear view of this warning. It does you no good to pretend you are not as
bad as other sinners—you are.

At the same time, notice the love and compassion that flows in, from,
and to the tragedy. Know that God can take any surrounding tragedy
and use it for your everlasting good if you would just look to Him. Allow
tragedies to point you toward where true and everlasting satisfaction can
be found—in Jesus Christ. Let it move you toward self-examination and
repentance. Jesus took all the sins and sorrows of this world down into
the grave and after defeating sin, Satan, and death, He rose. Jesus trium-
phed over evil. Seek Him.

Job 4:7; John 9:1-3

What then is Apollos?
What is Paul?

— 1 Corinthians 3:5

No matter what the stature or pedigree of a Christian is, that believer is a servant of God. Believers do not place their faith in anyone other than Jesus Christ. This includes the person who led you to Christ, the person who baptized you, and the person who discipled you. They are all only servants of the gospel. The reason this is important to highlight is because it is all too easy to focus on someone other than Christ. This does not diminish God's work through people, but a servant of God would prefer for you to focus on Jesus.

Turn away from the world and look to Jesus. Let Jesus alone be your most treasured possession. Direct your heart to imitate Jesus.

Ezekiel 37:15-28; John 17:20-23

'Who are you, Lord?'

— Acts 26:15

The non-essential details of your testimony will adapt to the different situations in which you proclaim them. But the unifying and central theme should never change: You once did not know who Jesus was, but now you do. You encountered the risen Jesus and have been given a calling. You once were blind, but now you see. You once were lost, but now you are found. You once had not received mercy, but now you have received mercy.

As you proclaim your faith, focus on Him and what He has done. Tell people what He is doing right now in your life. Talk about your future hope in Christ as well.

Isaiah 35:5; John 9:39

Who shall bring any charge against God's elect?
– Romans 8:33

Once God's verdict is set, it is secure. You are not liable to any outside accusation. No one—not even Satan himself—can successfully accuse you. By dying on the cross, Jesus conquered sin, Satan, and death. He redeemed you, saved you, and filled your life with hope. His death and resurrection began a new age. As God's elect, you are assured future glory. Only God is your judge, and Christ is your advocate.

What amazing comfort you have! What assurance of salvation you possess! What an amazing God you serve! Take refuge. Use this knowledge to flourish and thrive right now. Worship Him this day.

Isaiah 50:7-9; Romans 8:1

What agreement has the temple of God with idols?
– 2 Corinthians 6:16

You cannot combine the worship of the living God with worship of lifeless images. They are incompatible. Such simultaneous involvement is unimaginable to a Christian. Your old way of life is the way of death. Take care to walk in newness of life. Do not let the world bring you down or coerce you into its way. You must see the world for what it really is: dark, unfaithful, idolatrous, unjust, and hostile. Have no sort of partnership with the idols of this world. Rather, prefer to have the world against you than to have God displeased with you. Blessed are you when you ignore the voices of the disobedient and foolish people of this world, and instead follow the voice of the Good Shepherd calling you away from the cliff.

Leviticus 19:4; 1 Thessalonians 1:8-10

> *'Do you know how to discern the appearance of the sky,*
> *but cannot discern the signs of the times?'*
> — Matthew 16:3 (NASB)

By now, you should be able to discern God's work through Christ and the spiritual implications of it that are taking place all around you. You should be able to recognize divinely given signs that the kingdom of heaven is at hand, not just what the weather is going to be today or tomorrow.

Perhaps, though, you have all the information, signs, and wonders you need—but instead of recognizing them and applying them to your life, you stubbornly demand more signs and help. Pray for additional spiritual discernment. Close your ears to this world and spend more time reflecting on God's Word.

1 Chronicles 12:32; Matthew 12:38-42

SEPTEMBER 17

> *'Rabbi, when did you come here?'*
> — John 6:25

A crowd asks Jesus when he came, but they really want to know *how* he came. They still don't understand who Jesus is. Instead of being calmed and comforted by His presence, they are puzzled by Him. They are worried about details such as the date or time He arrived, how He came, and what He can do for them.

What matters, however, is who Jesus is. Once you understand that, the rest will fall into place. Keep this in mind as you proclaim the gospel and speak boldly with others. Don't get side-tracked with questions that don't confront them in new and important ways. They need to know *who* Jesus is. He comes from the Father. The Father sent Him for a purpose. That purpose includes people recognizing Jesus for who He really is; believing in Him; and obediently following Him.

As you talk with others and pose questions about who Jesus is to them, remind yourself of the answers. Remember who you are and what you are in Christ.

Isaiah 9:6; Philippians 2:6-11

'Now which of them will love him more?'
– Luke 7:42

Canceled debt is a symbol of God's forgiveness. The more debt that is canceled, the more gratitude a person typically has. One who has been forgiven much, loves much.

Jesus' inspired question here is designed to point you to this truth. Increased love results from increased forgiveness. Little love follows little forgiveness.

Therefore, come to Jesus humbly. Recognize your unworthiness. Understand your need for Him. Express your thanks regularly—or your gratitude is incomplete. *Isaiah 43:25; Ephesians 4:32*

'How long has this been happening to him?'
– Mark 9:21

You are at your wits' end. You have been struggling with something since you were a child. The condition you have is nothing new or temporary; it is old and chronic. Up to this point, you have felt helpless and vulnerable. You have tried this solution and that. You have gone to one person after another. No one has been able to cure you.

Nevertheless, what everyone else has failed to do, Jesus can do. He is all-powerful. He is compassionate. He is loving. And all things are possible for one who believes. This does not mean God is somehow obligated to do whatever you want. His healing may be different from what you pray for. The main truth here (and elsewhere) is that faith is critical, prayer is effective, and God is all-powerful—all of which you need to understand in light of Scripture. Understand God's Word and apply it to every detail of your life. *Isaiah 40:29-31; John 5:2-9*

But who are you, O man, to answer back to God? Will what is molded say to its molder, 'Why have you made me like this?'

— Romans 9:20

You are not in a position to challenge God. It is not only irreverent but also irrational. Feel free to bring all your questions, concerns, doubts, and fears to Him. But asking for answers is different from judging, accusing, or challenging Him. He is the Creator. He is your Creator. Even when His ways are not your ways, this fact remains. You would do good to accept whatever answer God may give you. God can deal with you however He chooses.

In humility and reverence, embrace this truth. God is just. God is righteous. God is love. God is judge. God is never wrong. Praise Him. Accept whatever answer God may give.

Psalm 115:3; Ephesians 1:3-6

'Men, you are brothers; why do you wrong each other?'

— Acts 7:26

Families should be loving and courteous toward each other, but some still fight. Thankfully, Christian ministry is about reconciliation with God and others. You are to be a peacemaker among people, even if they reject or do not appreciate you. As much as it depends on you, try to reconcile them in peace. Gently admonish them. Explain that what they are doing is wrong. Preach Jesus the Prince of Peace, who came to establish peace. Highlight our common heritage as believers. Pray fervently for God to reveal His peace to others as He has to you.

Leviticus 25:17; Matthew 18:21-35

'Why do you trouble the woman?'

— Matthew 26:10

Jesus' question is a rebuke of a disciple who disapproved of a woman's extravagant action of worship. He is reminding us not to quickly pronounce judgment on someone. The Holy Spirit may be prompting their action.

Without knowing it, you might be causing trouble or hardship in the midst of a good deed. What you regard as being inappropriate or a waste may have important wide-ranging implications. Even something as seemingly insignificant as a lovely gesture can have eternal significance. Instead, keep your focus on Jesus. Be captivated by Him. Think on the excellences and greatness of God. See everything from the perspective of eternity.

Psalm 91:14-16; Colossians 3:1

'Are you the teacher of Israel and yet you do not understand these things?'

— John 3:10

Instead of just feeding you answers, Jesus wants you to wake up and start thinking—especially if you have been reading the Bible for a long time like this teacher of Israel had. You may know the Scriptures well, but you must also understand what they reveal about Christ.

Cultivate the spiritual discipline of meditating on God's word. Slow down when reading it. Create a daily routine for doing it. Examine your understanding and respond, for true comprehension includes both understanding (the cognitive; rational; internal) and responding (the action; application; external). Always maintain a proper balance between your mind, heart, and will.

Deuteronomy 29:29; Acts 13:27

If we have sown spiritual things among you,
is it too much if we reap material things from you?
— 1 Corinthians 9:11

Beyond considering things conventionally and scripturally, consider them logically. Just as you pay for the physical (temporal) food you consume and are nourished by, be even more willing to provide financially for those who give you spiritual (everlasting) food for your benefit. There should not even be a second thought. Doing so is logical, as well as practical and scriptural.

What an amazing testimony it is to see the Apostle Paul giving up his personal rights to financial support for the sake of the gospel. How much more should you be willing to give up your rights when an opportunity arises? Always be ready and willing to exercise self-denial. Have the strength to submit to God.

Leviticus 19:13; Luke 10:1-12

'Tell us, when will these things be, and
what will be the sign when all these things
are about to be accomplished?'
— Mark 13:4

Maybe your expectations have not been met; impatience has set in; doubts are rising. Things are not what they seem. What you read in the Bible and see in the world appear to be two radically different and even opposing pictures.

In the original context, the disciples even stopped walking, sat down with Jesus, and asked Him this inspired question. One major point that Jesus makes in answering this question is that you should be ready, waiting, and watching expectantly for Him to return. Be on the lookout. He is returning, though you will not know when. Do not lie still at such a time as this. Fulfill your purpose. Lead a good life. Now, now is the time!

Isaiah 5:11-12; 1 Thessalonians 5:1-11

Then what becomes of our boasting? It is excluded.
By what kind of law? By a law of works?

— Romans 3:27

There is a natural tendency to think more highly of yourself then you ought to think. All too quickly, you can become prideful in your accomplishments. That pride can then develop into regarding your good works as the basis for God's gracious relationship with you. Eventually, you treat God as if He owes you something. The truth of the matter is, God owes you nothing.

Remember this often. Continue doing good things, but not because you think those good deeds will earn you merit with God. Instead of boasting about anything you have done, boast in Christ. Focus on what He accomplished. Put all your hope in Him.

Isaiah 10:15-19; Galatians 3:10-14

'But to what shall I compare this generation?'

— Matthew 11:16

'You're acting like a child!' That exclamation is not something you want to hear. Those types of statements typically point out someone's frustration and ill temper or highlight the person's unhappiness with whatever behavior they see in another person.

Jesus relates an entire generation to that of a child because entire generations can often act immaturely and childishly. He desires to draw individuals of every generation to Himself, but they often reject Him. In doing so, they reveal their selfish, unbelieving, and rejecting ways. They prefer a self-caressing religion.

Learn how to get rid of your foolish behaviors. Do all you can to avoid close fellowship with these sinful people and their ways. Steep yourself in God's Word. Respond how Jesus would respond.

Isaiah 57:20-21; Jude 10-13

> *'If it is my will that he remain until*
> *I come, what is that to you?'*
> – John 21:22

God does not make mistakes in calling people to do what He wants. Therefore, your curiosity about how He deals with other people is none of your business. Jesus will decide for them, as He will for you. You are called to follow Jesus wherever He leads *you*. Don't waste time trying to discern God's calling on everyone else's life; *you* follow Him.

These are Jesus' last words in John's gospel. Whatever role God calls you to play in His unfolding story of redemption, do it with all your might by the power of the Holy Spirit. As God the Father sent God the Son, now Jesus sends you to glorify God by making disciples. Go therefore! Make disciples. Baptize them. Teach them to obey all that Jesus has commanded you.

Proverbs 16:3; Galatians 6:4

> *Do you not know that we are to judge angels?*
> – 1 Corinthians 6:3

Even angels will be judged one day, and you will be involved in that process. 'So what?' you may ask. The main point of informing (or reminding) you of this is so that you will keep your daily affairs in proper perspective. If you are going to judge angels one day, you should all the more be able to handle earthly matters of business. To handle earthly matters, you need to be in close fellowship with other believers who will be doing the same thing.

Do not become like non-Christians who have no fear of God—which is the beginning of wisdom—and thus, have no clue how to manage daily activities and relationships according to God's Word. They will never judge angels. Instead, train yourself in godliness. Make use of temporary things but seek eternal things. Work honorably, as a workman who will not need to be ashamed on judgment day.

Daniel 7:22; Revelation 3:21

*'Does he thank the servant because he
did what was commanded?'*
— Luke 17:9

Do not expect God to congratulate you for doing something He expects you to do. The same applies when God instructs angels to do something, the apostles instruct the church to do something, or the government instructs citizens to do something.

You have a duty to perform. Granted, there are multiple motivations for obedience, but love is—and always should be—our highest motivation. But whenever our actions or thoughts are not founded on a higher motivation (such as love), a lesser motivation (such as duty) should automatically kick into high gear. In other words, you still need to do what needs to be done, when it needs to be done—whether you like it or not.

Micah 6:8; 1 Corinthians 7:17

October

'The same day Sadducees came to him,
who say that there is no resurrection,
and they asked him a question'

– Matthew 22:23

"And should not you have had mercy on your fellow servant, as I had mercy on you?"

— Matthew 18:33

When you point out someone else's mistakes, weaknesses, or flaws, remember that mercy is a two-way street. You are flawed and weak, as well. Listen to the words of Jesus: 'Blessed are the merciful, for they shall receive mercy.' Mercy is a characteristic of God. Therefore, mercy should be a characteristic of you, a follower of Jesus. When you do not show mercy, you cannot expect to receive it.

Contemplate the great and undeserved mercy you have received from God. Such generous, persistent, gentle, and proven love is all yours in Christ. He had mercy on you. Go and do likewise.

Zechariah 7:8-10; Ephesians 4:31-32

Do we then overthrow the law by this faith?

— Romans 3:31

The law was never a means of somehow 'earning' eternal life. But if people were only and always saved by faith, then it may seem logical to suggest that the law was only and always useless. The truth of the matter, however, is that the death and resurrection of Jesus Christ fulfills and confirms the law. The Law—as an expression of God's will—is most certainly still here.

Think about it. The law as a system is gone. It is 'off the books,' so to speak. It is fulfilled in the definitive and final sacrifice of Jesus Christ, who—as our high priest—lives to intercede for us. We are cleansed by the blood of the Lamb—Christ our Passover. Righteousness is available only through trusting in Jesus' work on the cross, but such faith must be expressing itself in love—in works of kindness—otherwise it may actually be dead.

Ask God to inscribe the fullness of His counsel—His instructions—in your innermost being. Read the Holy Scriptures. Trust what they teach. Practice your faith working through love—for grace does lead to transformation. Follow the example of righteous King Josiah, who turned to the LORD with all his heart, soul, and might, according to all the Law of Moses.

Jeremiah 31:31-34; Galatians 4:1-7

'Why do you delay?'
– Acts 22:16 (NASB)

God has been gracious to you. You have believed in Jesus. You are reconciled with God. Jesus has done everything for you—both now and forever—through your salvation. God now calls you to respond accordingly. He has given you the opportunity and responsibility to live a godly life. Part of that obedience includes baptism. You openly express your repentance towards God and faith in Jesus Christ. Not that baptism saves you, but God requires every believer to obey. Thus, baptism is not optional in the sense that Scripture gives you the choice depending on whether you feel like it.

Soberly recognize the seriousness of this lifelong commitment. Count the cost. Commit now to remaining faithful—for he who endures to the end will be saved. Don't delay. Get baptized today.

Exodus 19:5-6; 1 Peter 3:21-22

'And why do you not judge for yourselves what is right?'
– Luke 12:57

It is time for you to think and make a decision. Do not look to religious leaders. Do not look to your neighbors. Do not look to your family.

It is time now to decide what to do regarding Jesus. Therefore, soberly evaluate the times in which we live. Respond appropriately. Waiting could be disastrous. God's judgment is irreversible, and He and His holy Law are the standard of evaluation. Confirm your decision about following Jesus. Be sure of your relationship with Him. Do so now.

Deuteronomy 32:28-29; John 7:24

'Are grapes gathered from thornbushes,
or figs from thistles?'
– Matthew 7:16

There is a real and present danger in judging by outward appearances. They only reveal the surface of things. The true nature, character, and essence of something or someone will be revealed by what comes out of it or them. Similarly, your inner nature will ultimately express itself by the decisions you make and the actions you take. Your decisions will reveal your heart. As Jesus said, 'By their fruits you will know them.'

Many people have appeared to be a Christian without really being one. Think of Judas for a moment. The same can happen with teaching and doctrine. You might believe you are receiving the gospel and hearing biblical truth—only to find out later it was another gospel and an unbiblical teaching.

Examine yourself and what has come out of your thoughts and actions. As you do, you will see evidence that you are bearing much fruit, or you will not, if there is none. Yet don't mistake hundreds of blossoms as hundreds of fruits. They are not the same. Fruits take time and effort to be nurtured and grown. And no matter how amazing the blossoms may look, the only way they are ever going to produce fruit is if they are 'fertilized' by the transformative working of the Holy Spirit—enabling changes impossible on your own. To be a Christian means your very life and nature have changed. Merely saying and doing the right things are of no lasting value.

Don't be misled by appearances!

1 Samuel 16:6-7; James 2:14-26

'Do you see these great buildings?'
– Mark 13:2

Jesus wants to take your awe and wonder of things in this world and enlighten you with a different perspective. As magnificent and grandiose as many structures built by humans appear, their time is almost over. They will not stand firm forever. In fact, the magnificent display of any such monumental structural achievements—or even corresponding human achievements—ought to be seen in light of the coming destruction of this present evil world. God's judgment will soon fall on all great buildings—the cities of the nations will fall—and that will just be part of His coming judgments.

This world and everything in it is fleeting. Final judgment is coming. Hear the alarm bells ringing. Consider that you have but a little time to live. Persevere. Stand firm. Unlike the materials in this world, you will last forever. Live in light of this unshakeable truth.

2 Chronicles 36:17-21; Revelation 18

OCTOBER 7

For while there is jealousy and strife among you,
are you not of the flesh and behaving only in a human way?
– 1 Corinthians 3:3

Regardless of what you think about yourself or your situation, consider this truth: If you are envious and quarrelsome, you are living like an evil spirit! That self-centered behavior is similar to that of an unbeliever who does not have the gospel. There is no awareness of the value of confessing, 'It's my fault.' Instead of living that way, remember the spirit of adoption you received and live accordingly. God has nothing good to say about a belief that does not express itself in God-honoring behavior.

Seek to determine how the Lord would have you view and respond to each situation. Focus on the good and eternal. Move progressively from love of self to love of God. Every believer is necessary; and no one person can do everything. Treat others with respect. Value the work of others.

Proverbs 20:3; James 3:14-16

Are you so foolish?
Having begun by the Spirit,
are you now being perfected by the flesh?
– Galatians 3:3

Your flesh is unimpressed with everything you learn. It doesn't care. Therefore, you cannot start your Christian life by means of the Spirit and then try to finish the race on your own. The Holy Spirit did not just get you going so that you could continue racing on your own strength. Even if you are walking fast, you are making no progress without the Holy Spirit. Try running a marathon without water. You must continue by the Spirit in working out your own salvation with fear and trembling, for it is God who works in you, both to will and to work for His good pleasure. There are no other means by which to finish the race God has set out before you.

Therefore, remember how you started: by the Spirit. Examine your progression so far. Do not attempt to live another way, apart from the Spirit. Both your initiation and growth are due to the Spirit's work and are the result of faith.

Isaiah 44:1-5; Philippians 1:6

'*For which is greater, the gold or the temple*
that has made the gold sacred?'
– Matthew 23:17

You might be valuing things in reverse order or seeing them the wrong way: prioritizing the gifts above the Giver; or focusing on the objects in your presence over God's presence itself. Worldly commodities such as gold are not sacred without the presence of God. Everything that is truly holy, blessed, and purified derives its sanctity from God.

Consider right now what is genuinely sacred in your life. Treat the treasures that God has given you with the utmost respect but do not honor the treasures themselves. Instead, honor the Treasure-giver. Remember that you are always in the presence and sight of God.

Haggai 2:6-9; Revelation 21:18-27

*Listen, my beloved brothers, has not God chosen
those who are poor in the world to be rich in
faith and heirs of the kingdom, which he has
promised to those who love him?*

– James 2:5

Yes! But that does not mean that poverty equals faith. Rather, it is God's sovereign choice to grant strong faith to those who are deprived of worldly things. Of course, faith is still the key to inheriting the kingdom—here and elsewhere, regardless of the person's socio-economic status.

To be rich in faith, then, is to know God well. It is necessary to rely on God and obey His Word in all areas of your life. The poor have a great deal of experience relying on God, and often have a deeper understanding of God than those who have the privilege and distraction of wealth. Take your heart off the things of this world. Remember where your true citizenship is.

Psalm 37:10-11; Matthew 5:3

'Where is your faith?'

– Luke 8:25

Since Jesus is sovereign over all of creation, do not doubt His sovereignty over your life and situations. Faith is not merely an intellectual opinion or a mental assent. It is rooted in a practical confidence and dependence on God's supernatural power. Here, the miraculous power links to faith in Jesus. He has displayed His power and authority over creation. He controls nature.

What should be your response to His sovereign power over all the universe and all within it—including you? Trust God in and through every circumstance. He can and will carry you through. Never worry, for you have no right to.

Proverbs 27:1; Romans 8:28

Do you suppose, O man—you who judge those who
practice such things and yet do them yourself—that
you will escape the judgment of God?
– Romans 2:3

You may periodically compare yourself to certain people. Perhaps such a comparison makes you feel better about yourself. Other times, you feel worse. But no matter how good or bad you might feel you are in comparison to other people, God and His holy Law are the standard of holiness by which you will be judged. So remember this inspired question often. Determine to rid your life of the sins that are enslaving you. Be humble, not boastful and arrogant. Reflect on who God is and what He has done for you.

Psalm 62:11-12; Revelation 20:13

'O you of little faith,
why are you discussing among yourselves
the fact that you have no bread?'
– Matthew 16:8

Your discussions with people often reveal the condition of your faith. Certain discussions may even reveal a lack of faith—which would be surprising, given all that you have experienced in your relationship with Christ.

It should be impossible for you to worry about things. He alone is enough to calm your fears. He alone provides your needs. He alone sustains you. Nothing is too great for Him; no person too small. The fact of how much He has already blessed you—twice over—should be even more convicting.

Until you learn to live without fear, you will not find it easy to follow Jesus. Keep Him and His way of life before your eyes. Walk by faith; don't just speak more intelligently about your beliefs or experiences. Shift your focus. Trust in your heavenly Father instead of in yourself.

Psalm 78:18-22; Hebrews 5:11-13

'What must we do, to be doing the works of God?'
– John 6:28

It is natural for you to want something and to try to figure out a way of getting it. The problem, however, is that when it comes to eternal life you cannot earn it; it is a free gift you must accept. You have nothing to offer God toward earning your salvation. You don't just need help—you are empty handed without faith in Christ, and no matter how many 'works of God' you do apart from Him, they will not be enough.

Instead of focusing on yourself, wondering what you can do to earn God's favor, focus on Jesus. The works of God are not what God requires of you to gain eternal salvation. Listen to Jesus' answer to this question: 'This is the work of God, that you believe in him whom he has sent.' Upon believing, your good works are the necessary evidence and fruit of your new life as a believer—not the basis for your salvation.

Rejoice in Jesus and all His faithfulness. Say farewell to your past. Realize that it has been covered by the blood of Jesus. Learn to find your pleasure in Him. Remember your work of faith, labor of love, and steadfastness of hope in Jesus Christ.

Psalm 3:8; Romans 6:23

'Lord, to whom shall we go?'
– John 6:68

You now know that leaving Jesus is out of the question because there is no Plan B; no other option; no alternative gospel. Jesus has the words of eternal life. His doctrine is pure. The truth He speaks is of divine origin. He alone is Lord and Savior.

Thankfully, you recognize His life-giving words—even when others do not. You know His identity—even if others do not. And even when others do not believe, you do. Regretfully, destruction awaits those who go elsewhere, turning away from Christ. As for you, keep your commitment. Lay hold of it. Practice it. There are no shortcuts in the Christian life. Embrace your full salvation. Prevail and be triumphant.

Isaiah 44:6-8; Galatians 1:6-9

'What prevents me from being baptized?'
– Acts 8:36

The Bible speaks openly and positively about the benefits of identifying with Christ's death and resurrection through baptism. According to Scripture, baptism always accompanies or follows saving faith. Even if you have delayed, however, it is not too late. Take time now to address it. Then see to it that you are highlighting with other believers the Bible's emphasis on baptism. Teach them to obey all that the Lord has commanded.

Oh, what blessings await you and them!

2 Kings 5:10-14; Romans 6:4

'Why this waste?'
– Matthew 26:8

Your natural fallen instincts may put you at odds with Jesus. If you lack spiritual perception regarding what is going on around you, you may miss the right thing to say or do. Too often, we see and hear according to the flesh rather than according to the Spirit of God. You may be thinking about external matters rather than the spiritual reality taking place.

Therefore, do not act merely on impulses, instincts, and drives. Make a decision to change. Establish godly priorities. Reflect on the honor and reverence due your Creator and Lord. Do not waste your time, energy, and life holding on to more of this world than God calls you to. Use earthly necessities—food, clothing, shelter, and so on—for the spiritual advancement of yourself and others.

Genesis 14:17-24; John 19:38-42

> '*Will he not rather say to him,*
> "*Prepare supper for me, and dress properly,*
> *and serve me while I eat and drink,*
> *and afterward you will eat and drink*"?'
> – Luke 17:8

As Christ's servant, it doesn't matter how tired you are, you still need to do what you are told without expecting to be thanked for it. This may be hard to hear and an unwelcome guide for discipleship, especially to our modern ears. The chosen comparison almost makes God out to be like a restaurant owner who requires his employees to delay taking their lunch break until the patrons are taken care of first. But the overall point is spot on. The best you can do is still less than what you owe God. You can never make God your debtor. By working hard and staying faithful, you cannot earn your way into His favor since you are only doing what you were created to do. At the same time, there is no place for complacency in discipleship.

Therefore, break up any fallow ground in your life. Lay aside all selfishness. Treat others with respect. Focus on God. Serve and please Him. Seek His praise alone—not that of others.

2 Samuel 12:20; Revelation 14:13

For when one says, 'I follow Paul,'
and another, 'I follow Apollos,'
are you not being merely human?
— 1 Corinthians 3:4

Internal cliques, artificial rivalries, and human-made divisions are all ungodly and deceptive in the church. If you are a Christian, then you are united with other believers in Christ. Regardless of what pastor you have, what church you attend, or what believers you are in close fellowship with, there is only one Christ. When these characteristics of your group merely reflect secular trends, they do not necessarily promote love or exalt Christ. Even worse is any type of 'in-group' belittling of others.

Be watchful. Do not set yourself up on a pedestal. Do not try to impress others. Do not use the truth to promote yourself. Edify one another. Reject any boasting, divisiveness, or power plays. Instead, elevate Jesus. Proclaim the sufficiency of the cross.

Deuteronomy 33:2-4; Philippians 2:2-3

'He has a demon, and is insane; why listen to him?'
— John 10:20

Spiritual concerns can seem odd to an unbelieving world. Many of your claims no doubt seem outlandish to non-Christians; indeed, even upsetting. You may even be called all sorts of names: fanatic, radical, weird, insane, demonic, and similar insults. Naturally, that is all almost anyone can say when they don't understand who Jesus is, where He comes from, or what He teaches.

You, on the other hand, know Jesus and hear His voice. You understand that demons destroy and abandon, but Jesus saves and heals. You know demons harm, but Jesus helps. You can have great confidence, then, when you hear His voice. Listen for it. Be discerning. Read the Bible. Consider what He expects from you. Seek daily times of solitude. Imagine standing before Him. Deliberately communicate with Him.

Hosea 4:6; Acts 4:5-12

OCTOBER 21

'How can you speak good, when you are evil?'
– Matthew 12:34

Jesus exposes a person's true identity: An evil heart can only speak forth evil. Not that the words are necessarily bad or evil, but the motives and orientation will always be wrong from a wicked heart. Anything that is not from faith is something that the Bible compares to the chaff from the harvesting of grain that blows away in the wind, something that is worthless.

Similarly, your speech reveals a lot about you. Your words and actions reveal your heart. In fact, your heart is the barometer of your soul, as implied here and made explicit elsewhere. Your heart's uncontrolled passions will be your greatest hindrance to knowing God, others, and yourself.

Schedule a set time each day to examine your heart. Select a quiet and private place. Pour out your concerns, doubts, and fears to God. With others, speak of what nourishes one's spiritual life. Discuss spiritual things that lift you above the things of this world. Have heavenly conversations. Guard against unnecessary or trivial speech.

Psalm 59:11-13; James 3:10-12

OCTOBER 22

Do you not know that in a race all the runners run, but only one receives the prize?
– 1 Corinthians 9:24

Get in the game. Compete. Win the prize. Yes, this will require self-control and much effort. This will entail dying to yourself; loosening your grip on the rights, freedoms, and desires you may hold dear. But there is no point even entering the race if you are not going to try to win. You need to pursue Christ in such a way that you will ultimately get the prize.

Whatever it takes, become the person God has called you to be so that you will obtain an incorruptible reward. Stop chasing after empty dreams and pursue God's truth. Be concerned if you ever stop growing and developing. Do not squander your time, but make the most of every opportunity.

Jeremiah 29:13; Matthew 6:33

'O faithless generation, how long am I to be with you?
How long am I to bear with you?'

– Mark 9:19

Notice that Jesus does not just ask how long He will be with them, but how long He can put up with them. Anyone's unwillingness to take God at His word and to only consider what is humanly possible reveals a lack of faith. Jesus' righteous anger with such human nearsightedness triggers this inspired question, which Jesus applies to the whole generation.

In fact, the greatest danger in life for every generation is unbelief—refusing to trust God. Demonstrate your trust today in some way: perhaps by laying aside your plans and expectations, giving sacrificially, waiting patiently, following unwaveringly, or trusting wholeheartedly. Whatever it is, commit yourself to at least one specific response today.

Deuteronomy 32:5; Hebrews 11:6

'What is the kingdom of God like?
And to what shall I compare it?'

– Luke 13:18

You may wonder how God is establishing His kingdom today. As you look around and in many places, His kingdom may seem unremarkable. You may have expected to see greater glory and power then you currently do.

But just wait. One day, the kingdom of God will surpass anything you could have ever imagined. Although Jesus' ministry started off small, it has grown to impact the whole world and will continue to do so until He returns. It includes and incorporates all nations. All heaven and earth will be changed. Praise God for the fact that you are His and in the kingdom. You are destined for glory. Contemplate such a destiny and get ready for it. Let this be your ambition. Pray, 'Thy kingdom come!'

Isaiah 40:18-31; Matthew 13:31-32

"Why do you stand here idle all day?"
— Matthew 20:6

You may experience times in your life when you cannot find work. The lack of success does not necessarily mean you are lazy. It does not necessarily mean there is a problem with you. Sometimes employers make final decisions based on worldly interests or impure motives. You may begin to think that you do not have the best contacts, or that you do not have the best looks, or that you do not have tremendous financial resources to wait out the time without work.

The good news is that even if you are passed over by everyone else, Jesus provides you with equal opportunity to receive full rewards in the kingdom of God. Be encouraged. Wait upon God. Work diligently. Render thanks to God for the gifts you have already received, and will someday receive.

Psalm 145:9; Romans 2:11

If even lifeless instruments, such as the flute or the harp, do not give distinct notes, how will anyone know what is played? And if the bugle gives an indistinct sound, who will get ready for battle?
— 1 Corinthians 14:7-8

You cannot just run your fingers over the strings of an instrument and assume you are making music. Sounds may be heard, but they will not make sense. You need a melody. You need distinct notes, or no one will know what you are playing. If they cannot determine what you are playing, they cannot respond appropriately. They will not enjoy or benefit from your music. Similarly, the body of Christ will not be edified if everyone is the same as you. We need diversity.

Embrace the gifts and opportunities God gives you in order to serve Him and other people. Allow others to do the same. Take heed. Encourage one another. Enjoy one another. Stay accountable.

2 Chronicles 5:11-14; Hebrews 13:1

Has God rejected his people?
– Romans 11:1

God never lies. Just because some Jews reject Jesus does not mean God rejects all Jews. In fact, even to this day, there are Jews who believe in Jesus! And they are already experiencing some of the blessings of God's ancient promises to them—though, as with Gentiles, not yet fully experiencing such blessings until Christ returns. These Jewish Christians' belief in the same Jesus we worship testifies to God's faithfulness to His people. God's character shines through His faithfulness—He never abandons His people. Rather, He continues to guarantee their ultimate redemption and restoration.

Pause for a moment to thank and praise God for being so faithful, trustworthy, and merciful. If you remain in Christ, you will never be rejected. In Christ, God's grace will always exceed your sin. Oh, what sweetness is yours in Christ!

Psalm 94:14-15; 1 Corinthians 10:32-33

'Is not this the carpenter's son? Is not his mother called Mary? And are not his brothers James and Joseph and Simon and Judas?'
– Matthew 13:55

You may know people who assume Jesus is nothing special. They know about His family and where He comes from. They hear about Him doing ordinary things other people also do, such as teaching. They might think, 'What is so great about Him?'

This type of familiarity all too often breeds contempt. Perhaps new experiences and recent events will ultimately challenge their opinions. They may even acknowledge that Jesus is exceptional; that He is amazing; and even that He is powerful. But they still end up rejecting Him.

View their comments as an opportunity to proclaim your testimony. Remember what you used to think and how you would react. Be kind, not rough or harsh. Be patient, not quick-tempered. Rely on God.

Isaiah 53:1-3; John 1:9-13

For why should my liberty be determined
by someone else's conscience?
– 1 Corinthians 10:29

The guiding principle in your Christian life should not be your personal liberty, but the glory of God. Your freedom cannot become an obstacle for an unbeliever. Your testimony must testify to the exclusivity of Christ—for He is the only way. It is all too easy to rationalize your freedom in Christ, make excuses, or lie to yourself. Granted, your conscience is a God-given guide—but it is fallible.

Therefore, gauge the motives behind your actions. Get to the heart of the issue. Desire and seek God's pleasure and your neighbor's well-being above your own. Be mindful of others. Create a reputation of putting others above yourself. Be a role model of godliness.

Psalm 15; Philippians 2:1-11

'Teacher, what shall we do?'
– Luke 3:12

People will ask you what they need to do when you proclaim God's unwavering message of being productive and bearing much fruit. It is one thing to share a prophecy or discuss things that will happen in the end times, but it is quite another thing to exhort someone and give them practical wisdom in their daily life.

People who claim to know God but do not live for Him are like unfertile trees that will be cut down. You know that God expects faith-filled believers to act on that faith by living out their commitment to Him by doing good works out of the fear of God and love for Him. So take care to influence all who encounter you in a way geared towards introducing them to God. Give a balanced presentation (like two bicycle wheels) of the truths of God. Fulfill the divine mission of reaching the world with His grace.

Ezekiel 18:25-29; Acts 16:25-34

But what does it say?

– Romans 10:8

The message is clear—and it is clearly amazing. Righteousness is based on faith. You do not need a telescope or microscope to find it. No journey is needed. No amount of good works can earn it. The righteousness of God is yours in Christ. Faith alone in Jesus Christ's completed work of salvation saves.

Therefore, enjoy this free gift. Live in a holy way consistent with this truth. Pursue righteousness.

Habakkuk 2:4; Galatians 2:20

November

'Now while the Pharisees were gathered together,
Jesus asked them a question'

– Matthew 22:41

What more shall I say?
— Hebrews 11:32

Even though you only have abbreviated stories and limited lists of all the saints who have gone before you, consider their lives. Their gospel message and godly actions matched, and it was a glorious thing. We rightly honor them for their faith and faithfulness. They lived knowing that this world is not all that there is. Their testimonies give us hope. They suffered faithfully.

Now, draw both inspiration and instruction from them. Recognize that the same God that gave them strength to live the way they did can do the same for you. Resolve to leave the legacy of a godly life.

Job 1:8; Acts 21:13

'Why do you speak to them in parables?'
— Matthew 13:10

Many people think Jesus' teaching is cryptic. They wonder why Jesus does not just spell everything out for them. Part of the reason is so that you will explore and seek out the deeper meaning in His words that the Holy Spirit gives to those who receive Him.

The truth and explanations of divine revelation are yours for the gleaning. They are visible, evident, and meaningful to you as a believer. They give you insight into God's kingdom. To others, however, they remain a mystery and do not illustrate eternal realities. Yet there is more going on than just some abstract truths. God is still accomplishing things in this world through Jesus' death and resurrection.

Spend quality time with Him. Listen with humility. Seek what is true, interior, and eternal. Value these things.

Lamentations 3:55-66; Ephesians 4:17-24

'Whose likeness and inscription is this?'
– Mark 12:16

Your relationship with the government connects to your relationship with God. God institutes governments and teaches us to be subject to them. Therefore, Jesus points out this truth of submitting to the government by asking this inspired question. You should give to someone what bears their image—that is, give to Caesar what is Caesar's.

Even more, you should give to God what bears His image: you! Submit every aspect of your life to Him—including your participation in the political process, whatever that might look like where you live. Submit to the governing authorities from a position of love for country and respect toward God's appointed servants. Bear fruit with patience. Present yourself to God as a living sacrifice.

Genesis 1:26-27; Romans 13:1-7

What am I to do?

— 1 Corinthians 14:15

It is time to ask yourself this inspired question about your corporate worship, because your mind might not be benefiting even if your spirit leaves encouraged. Both need to be edified in worship with others. You regularly need to pray with both your mind and spirit. God inspires both.

Likewise, you need to remember outsiders. If only your spirit is encouraged, you have nothing to proclaim to someone else except an emotion you experienced. In turn, it can sometimes seem to people that God does not really care about the things that worry them: kids, health, finances, and so forth. In other words, you must not base your relationship with God on emotions, feelings, and experiences. He knows exactly what you need and (far less importantly) what you want. On countless occasions, the great men and women of faith have surrendered their own emotions and desires to God. We, too, must keep our minds disciplined to follow God's instructions, even when our heart may be deceitfully leading us towards another path.

Therefore, cast your cares, concerns, and fears on Him. Engage your spirit and mind. He cares for all of you. Nothing is outside His control. Certainly, you may have good reasons to be concerned, but God gives you even better reasons to trust Him, grow spiritually, and think of others.

Zephaniah 3:9; Romans 14:19

How can we who died to sin still live in it?
— Romans 6:2

One way to gauge your spiritual growth is to assess your daily attempts to mortify sin. Yes, you are declared righteous. Jesus has set you free. Jesus has saved you from the power of sin in your life. But willfully living in sin is incompatible with being a true Christian. It is impossible for a genuine believer to stay in a lifestyle of sin with no remorse and repentance.

A healthy spiritual life, where you can enjoy peace and comfort, depends on you regularly putting to death the sin that indwells you. This is your daily and long-term task accomplished only by means of the Holy Spirit. The moment you stand still in your fight against sin, you will be beaten down by it. You are in a constant spiritual warfare.

Don't just hide your sins better. Deal with them. Don't just treat the symptoms—address the illness. Don't just try to control sin—utterly uproot it from your life. Render sin ineffective. Rise up against it—with all your strength!

Psalm 16:8; 1 John 3:4-10

'Is it lawful to divorce one's wife for any cause?'
— Matthew 19:3

Thinking you can do whatever you want, whenever you want, and however you want—not to mention for any reason you want—reveals how hard your heart is. Eventually, you may question whether Jesus is more restrictive than you believe or whether He tolerates opinions that are in tune with what the world judges as being OK.

At those moments, remember that the person who loves the most sees into your soul, and therefore recognizes and understands the greatest dangers. Jesus—that One who loves you the most—sees what others do not. He speaks the truth—even when most people do not want to hear it. He understands people are in love with their own opinions and that their hearts are hard.

Use this inspired question to address any hardness in your heart. Flee self-love, self-will, and self-interest. Pursue the glory of God.

Malachi 2:13-16; Hebrews 13:4

*'If then God gave the same gift to them
as he gave to us when we believed in the
Lord Jesus Christ, who was I that I
could stand in God's way?'*

– Acts 11:17

We are all equal in Christ. The same Spirit that you received, every other believer receives, as well. We share a common faith in Jesus. There is only one Spirit. If you ever stand in the way of other people becoming full members of the Body of Christ, you are standing in direct opposition to God Himself, who called them.

Beware of challenging God's revealed will. Do not strive against Him. Instead, remember that God is sovereign over everyone and in control of everything. Build up one another. Edify and embrace one another.

Jonah 3; Galatians 2:7-10

'Why do you question in your hearts?'

– Luke 5:22

Jesus knows what you are thinking. He knows your thought process. He knows your heart. He asks this inspired question to challenge you directly. And the question concerns why you would question Him.

One way you can examine yourself is to ask whether your question is a form of adoration or challenge. Why are you asking why, for example? Do you trust Him? Be unlike those who do not know God. Show respect and reverence. Do not be proud. Find ways to cultivate a more receptive heart. Make every effort to understand your motives, so that you may be kept humble.

1 Chronicles 28:9; Matthew 9:4

> *'Then what sign do you do, that we may see and*
> *believe you? What work do you perform?'*
>
> – John 6:30

The demand for a sign often reveals a desire to control God. You are discontented with what you have already received, and so you insist on having a continuous supply of blessings. This inspired question reveals that people are quick to come to Jesus for the food and goodies without making the commitment to believe and follow Him. If they were really looking for a sign, they would have recognized the One they just saw. In the end, their bellies were full—but their souls were still empty.

Take time to recognize the signs He has already given you. Keep a journal. Say with the apostle Paul, 'In any and every circumstance, I have learned the secret of facing plenty and hunger, abundance and need. I can do all things through him who strengthens me.' That is the secret to true contentment.

Ezekiel 20:10-13; Matthew 27:39-44

> *Let me ask you only this: Did you receive the Spirit*
> *by works of the law or by hearing with faith?*
>
> – Galatians 3:2

By works or by faith? That is the question. There is no third option. You first came to experience God's Spirit by hearing with faith. To understand it any differently is to forsake the gospel. The gospel is not merely about making bad people good, but about making dead people live. It cannot be reduced to mere moral improvement or behaviorism: 'Quit this and stop that.' The bigger issue is whether you are indeed in Christ—experiencing a personal relationship with Him. Those other things apply and are true, but you receive the Spirit by hearing with faith. The Spirit confirms your conversion, which was by grace through faith alone. The Spirit is your down-payment that you belong to God. The moment you believed the gospel, you received the Holy Spirit. You did not earn the gift of the Holy Spirit because of your works. Simple belief opened the door to receiving the Spirit. Receiving the Spirit was all about faith, and faith came from hearing. Praise God!

Joel 2:28-32; Romans 10:17

If God is for us, who can be against us?
— Romans 8:31

In Christ, God is for you. He is working out all things for you. Nothing can come between you and His love. This does not mean life will be easy. This does not mean everyone will be your friend. This does not mean your career, income, or prestige will be all that you desired. But ultimately, nothing can separate you from the love of God in Christ. No one can take away your salvation in Christ, for God Himself has established it. His love for you is truly that great.

No matter what difficulties you face right now or in the future, the love of God in Christ abides with you. Meditate on this truth. Nourish those around you with it. Replace any ingratitude with gratitude. Thank Him for His love. Stand firm in the faith.

Isaiah 54:17; Hebrews 13:5-6

'What is written in the Law?
How do you read it?'
— Luke 10:26

Jesus wants you to reflect on what the Law requires: Love God and love your neighbor. There is no limit to your obligation to love both. Your love ought to be comprehensive, all-embracing, and far-reaching. There is no place for racism, bigotry, or hateful prejudice in such love.

Look to God and trust His Word, not your culture, tradition, or understanding. Choose only the things that will best help you attain the end goal for which you were created in Christ: good works. Get off to the right start today. Grow in service.

Joshua 22:5; 1 Thessalonians 1:2-3

> *The cup of blessing that we bless, is it not a*
> *participation in the blood of Christ?*
> *The bread that we break, is it not a participation*
> *in the body of Christ?*
> — 1 Corinthians 10:16

Idolatry is a real danger. You may think it is just a word used to scare people away from anything not pertaining to God, but there are real evil forces, demonic powers, and satanic influences. With that in mind, by participating in the Lord's Supper you are receiving the numerous provisions and benefits of the New Covenant. It is unimaginable that you would participate in and accept any other pagan ceremonial meal's symbolism as your own. Why even flirt with such idols? Treat them as infectious diseases or as contagious viruses.

You cannot be fickle here. You cannot bounce around or switch back and forth between Christ and evil forces. If you play with fire it will burn you! You need to fully embrace and enjoy a central aspect of being united with Christ: the body (bread) and blood (cup) of Christ. Do not get distracted. Set aside time to prepare yourself for communion. Be faithful.

Psalm 116:12-14; Mark 14:22-25

> *'"Lord, when did we see you hungry and feed*
> *you, or thirsty and give you drink?"'*
> — Matthew 25:37

As a Christian, our Lord calls you to help those in need—especially those in the family of faith. You cannot ignore them. In fact, not only are you meeting a human need, but the object of your loving action is Jesus Himself.

How you treat others is one significant way to gauge the state of your heart. It is an indication of your genuine relationship with Jesus, for the expression of the Christian life is the work of loving others.

Go and show mercy. Be compassionate. Be proactive. Use your money and resources for the greatest purposes on earth: godliness, giving, and God's glory. See people from a new perspective and in a different way.

Leviticus 19:33-34; 3 John 5-8

'And if you have not been faithful in that which is another's, who will give you that which is your own?'
– Luke 16:12

Jesus' question comes after His parable of a dishonest but shrewd servant whose master has entrusted him to manage his wealth. The lesson is this: If you cannot faithfully manage someone else's things, there's no reason to believe you can handle your own things. If you are not responsible in this life with what God has given you, then how good a steward will you be in the life to come? Remember that to turn God's grace into a license for immorality would be to deny our only Master and Lord, Jesus Christ

Take a moment to really learn this great and fundamental lesson. Your faithfulness now prepares you for the life to come. It even helps determine how many blessings you will possess in the age to come. Be all the more faithful right now so that you will be given an even greater reward in the life to come. Cleanse yourself from anything that is dishonorable. Recall and respond to the words of Jesus your Savior: 'Well done, good and faithful servant. You have been faithful over a little; I will set you over much. Enter into the joy of your master.'

Hosea 2:8; 1 Peter 1:4-5

'But who do you say that I am?'
– Mark 8:29

Let this question sink into your soul. In contrast to what every person in this world who does not personally know Jesus says about Him, Jesus expects a more accurate and adequate answer from you. The difference between how you answer and that of popular opinion ought to be profound. Regardless of what any unbeliever says about Jesus, a better answer is still needed. It is your responsibility to supply the answer God has given you.

God has entrusted you with the mysteries of His kingdom. He has given you spiritual eyes to evaluate His significance. You have a personal relationship with Him. Therefore, proclaim the truth about Jesus.

Now reread the question. Spend time reflecting on how you will respond.

Exodus 3:13-17; John 12:37-43

'Do you believe this?'

— John 11:26

Jesus doesn't just ask if you believe, but whether you believe 'this.' The account here quotes Him asking a specific question about whether someone believes He can bring a person who has passed away back to life. But in a larger sense, He is asking whether a person believes He is capable of granting not just physical life but eternal life. And He's not simply seeking for your statement of affirmation—a yes or no.

Rather, He wants you to give Him a thoughtful answer. He wants you to reflect, understand, and make a decisive, life-changing decision. Do you believe 'this,' that Jesus is the resurrection (though you die, you will live again) *and* the life (everlasting)? As a believer, you will be raised imperishable. He guarantees you eternal life.

Believe it. Repeat it aloud or in your mind. Before time began, God purposed to share the promised gift of eternal life. Realize that you are an heir of God. Your past is gone. All your sins have been forgiven once and for all. Say to yourself today, 'It is finished, covered by the blood of Jesus.'

Joel 3:17-21; Acts 24:14-21

*'For which is greater, the gift or the altar that
makes the gift sacred?'*
– Matthew 23:19

No gift is sacred apart from God. His presence alone makes the gift sacred. Keep this in mind when you present something in worship. Your offerings—praise, money, good deeds, service projects—derive their sanctity from the place where God's presence dwells.

Sadly, superficiality steadily strikes—and you may quickly lose focus. Thoughtlessness versus mindfulness might seem like a small distinction, but it makes all the difference. Sadly, you can become so familiar with the ritualistic aspects of worship that you might even risk taking the name of God in vain if praying in an overly rote, casual way or singing familiar worship songs and hymns in a mechanical, thoughtless way. Worshiping God in a superficial (rather than mindful) way can result from (and result in) your quickly losing focus. Yet 'I am a great King,' God says, 'and My name is to be feared.'

Evaluating spiritual things inaccurately dishonors God. Treating something sacred as if it is common, or vice versa, treating something common as if it has some sacred value, both invoke God's judgment. Take time to evaluate material things appropriately. Do not practice your faith mechanically. Pursue godliness.

Isaiah 66:1-2; Acts 17:22-31

> *'Men of Israel, why do you wonder at this, or*
> *why do you stare at us,*
> *as though by our own power or piety we have*
> *made him walk?'*
> — Acts 3:12

The One responsible for healing someone is the risen Lord, not you. Therefore, you must remember to redirect someone's attention away from you and onto the Lord. Any unnecessary attention drawn to you undermines God's glory. Do not let people stand in awe of you. Correct their misunderstanding. Divine healing points to the saving power of Jesus—that is why there is no reason for people to marvel at what they believe is your power. God raised up Jesus. There is nothing miraculous beyond His ability. Be like Joseph or Daniel: Give Him all the honor and praise.

Isaiah 43:11; 1 Corinthians 2:1-5

> *Do you want to be shown, you foolish person,*
> *that faith apart from works is useless?*
> — James 2:20

You can imagine that most people probably would not want to find out that James' statement is true: Faith apart from works is, indeed, useless. The test of whether or not one has *both* faith *and* works would incriminate many. You cannot separate them. It is foolishness. As the old saying goes, 'Faith that doesn't work doesn't work.' A fruitless life necessarily suggests that someone does not belong to God. A fruitful life, by contrast, brings glory to God.

Putting faith into practice is what counts. It is a living—not a dead, passive, or indifferent—faith. Whatever you say, if it does not have corresponding actions, does not matter. Works are an evidence of true faith. Strive to become more like Christ and to become more effective in doing good works for Christ. Walk in fellowship with Him.

Ezekiel 33:30-33; Romans 1:5-6

'If then you are not able to do as small a thing as that,
why are you anxious about the rest?'

– Luke 12:26

Worrying accomplishes nothing. In fact, it reveals a lack of trust. Since you cannot even add a little bit of time to your life, there is no need to worry about other things that are beyond your control. You will waste much of your energy on worrying rather than directing it toward things that you do have control over, such as serving God and caring for others. God knows what you need and want, and He can provide. Stop worrying. He loves you deeply. Put your hope in Him and His promises. You can entrust Him with all your worries.

1 Samuel 30:6; Philippians 4:6

'Which commandment is the first of all?'

– Mark 12:28 (NRSV)

In the Bible account, a scribe has asked Jesus to identify a 'first commandment'—not first in order, but first in importance. Jesus answers by summarizing all the commandments that deal with a person's direct relationship with God and other people, because a follower of Christ has responsibilities to both. You must love God with all your being and love everyone you encounter as yourself. His answer summarizes the Ten Commandments.

Of course, though, just knowing the right answer does not mean you are in good standing with God, as Jesus tells the scribe: 'You are not far from the kingdom of God.' His answer suggests the scribe is close but must go farther—and so must you.

Embrace this great commandment and live it out in practice. Be deliberate. Devise ways to measure how you are doing. Do not rely upon your works, but test your life by them.

1 Kings 8:54-61; James 2:8

Or do you not know that he who is joined to a
prostitute becomes one body with her?

— 1 Corinthians 6:16

You are free to choose what you wish, but you are not free to choose the consequences. God created everything for a purpose, even your sexual organs. What you do with your entire body matters and it will have consequences in the afterlife.

Therefore, you need to use your body in the right way and for the right purpose. Any illicit sexual union is incompatible with your union with Christ and matters both now and in the future. You belong to Christ. You are part of His body. You cannot wed Christ to someone who is not part of Christ as you are. There is no such thing as a casual sexual encounter or a friend with benefits. Each sexual encounter involves all of you—physically and spiritually—not just a part.

Address these dangers today. Battle temptation. Be concerned if you do not. Remember that you were bought with a price. Honor God with your body—inside and out.

Proverbs 6:20-35; Romans 6:5-11

*'How is it that you fail to understand that I
did not speak about bread?'*
– Matthew 16:11

There comes a time to stop and address any misunderstandings you may have. Maybe your focus remains only at the level of material blessings. Maybe you only concentrate on how God's intervention pertains to your physical needs. In doing so, you do not notice or understand the more important spiritual truths that all of God's works convey.

There is deeper meaning to discern. It is time to encounter God's goodness directly rather than through His blessings. Experiencing God's material blessings will not necessarily activate a proper response from you—even if we recognize how miraculous they are. Directly experiencing His divine presence—an experience that is utterly intoxicating—will.

Seek out His presence. Deepen your walk by regaining a spiritual perspective. Respond specifically by way of faith, worship, praise, thanksgiving, or prayer.

Ezekiel 12:1-2; 2 Timothy 2:7

November 25

But what is God's reply to him?
— Romans 11:4

There may come a time when you feel isolated, as if you are the only Christian around. It may come after a move to a new place. It may come simply when you are reading or watching the news. Being a true believer can seem lonely at times and can even lead to feelings of frustration, fear, and hopelessness. But God's Word reveals that He has always preserved a remnant of people as evidence of His faithfulness. No matter how hopeless things may appear, God will continue to sustain and maintain a body of believers.

So be encouraged. Do not let your present feelings harm your judgment. Attend church regularly. Join activities when you can. Prayerfully seek for others who are passionate for Christ. God will provide.

1 Kings 19:9-18; Revelation 12:17

November 26

'Were not ten cleansed? Where are the nine?'
— Luke 17:17

The question here doesn't really demand an answer. Surely, Jesus doesn't want to know the exact location of everyone who did not express gratitude. The point of asking this inspired question was to help the one who did return to realize the spiritual meaning of what was going on. Jesus had commanded that they observe the letter of the law—that they go to the priest, as the law required. But His love takes you beyond the bare minimum physical requirements. He wants a relationship with you.

Many people receive divine blessings, but few show their gratitude. Like the lepers, you too have been cleansed (from sin!). You too have experienced God's love and mercy. But you should not be like most people, who do not respond appropriately. Nothing prevents them from expressing appreciation, for they are capable. Yet they do not praise God as they should. They don't proclaim His role in blessing them.

Do your best to respond appropriately to each blessing God gives you. Many people might miss the moment, but you should not. Thank God today!

Psalm 106:13; Romans 1:21

'Do you not yet perceive? Do you not remember the five loaves for the five thousand, and how many baskets you gathered?'

– Matthew 16:9

Forgetting God's past acts in your life is all too easy as you continue in the hustle and bustle of life. Failing to grasp what those acts reveal about Jesus is even easier if you don't pause to reflect upon them. In fact, the word 'remember' here means more than just recalling past events or facts. It means concentrating long and hard on what has taken place, gleaning insights from it, and renewing your faith.

Divine acts in your life ought to increase your spiritual awareness. They should highlight who Jesus is. They should clarify His mission for you and be easy to recall. Don't be so preoccupied with earthly things that you forget God's generous provisions (both past and present). Harvest some spiritual insights by reflecting on this inspired question according to God's Word.

Numbers 14:11; Hebrews 4:2

'What then will this child be?'

– Luke 1:66

Some local fears and regional reports regarding events that are taking place may give you strong and deep emotional reactions. You, as well as others, might wonder what role someone will have in God's plan (whether a presidential candidate, potential spouse, or new pastor). It is clear that God is doing something. It is clear that someone specific is His chosen instrument. But questions still abound. Expectations are numerous. The future seems unclear.

Consult the Lord. Discuss with a fellow believer what has been heavy on your heart and soul. Study and meditate upon the Scriptures. Always return to this basic principle: God gives wisdom.

Isaiah 7:14; Ephesians 1:7-10

> *'Which one of you convicts me of sin?*
> *If I tell the truth, why do you not believe me?'*
> — John 8:46

Jesus is above reproach. His doctrine is accurate. His life is flawless. No one has ever had legitimate evidence to accuse Him of anything. Therefore, instead of slandering Him, everyone should believe in Him. If He is not false, He is true. If He is not a liar, He is a truth proclaimer. If He is not a sinner, He is sinless.

Knowing that Christ is sinless and speaks the truth, continue believing and trusting in Him. Hold on to Him. Observe all that He commands. Do what He has told you to do.

Jeremiah 11:9-13; Hebrews 7:26-29

> *'But how then should the Scriptures be*
> *fulfilled, that it must be so?'*
> — Matthew 26:54

God is in charge. His Word will be fulfilled. There is no need for you to try to prevent God's will from happening—perhaps even in death—if God has already decreed it. Whatever affliction, unrest, or uncertainty remains in your life, God is still in control. Cry out to Him. Nothing happens by chance. God can even use the evil plans of ungodly people to advance His purposes and fulfill His declared will. Jesus knew this all too well. He knew God's plan and fulfilled it. Jesus knew and lived the Scriptures.

Examine your calling today. Faithfully fulfill the roles God has given you. Lay hold of the hope set before you. Remember that the righteous cry out, and the Lord hears, and delivers them out of all their troubles. Fear not!

Joshua 21:43-45; Romans 15:4

December

*'And no one was able to answer him a word,
nor from that day did anyone dare to
ask him any more questions.'*

– Matthew 22:46

'What then shall we do?'

– Luke 3:10

Seeing how radically different your life is and how God is working through you, people will want to know how they might also have a new beginning. They see corruption and injustice all around them, but you are telling them there is a better way. Not only do you tell them what they should already know—play by the rules, do not exploit your position of authority over people, promote greater equality—but even more importantly, you point them to King Jesus. In Him are ultimate justice, ultimate hope, and ultimate resurrection.

Do everything you can to bring people to Christ. Improve your conversations with others. Believe that God can use your words as He Himself draws people to Himself. Make a difference. Have faith that you will.

Ezekiel 18:5-9; Acts 2:37-41

December 2

For who hopes for what he sees?

– Romans 8:24

Hope is an important aspect of the Christian faith. You eagerly wait for something you cannot see right now. It began the moment you believed. Maybe that has been a long time. Perhaps it is still new. Either way, the full extent of your salvation will not be experienced this side of heaven—for although you 'have been saved,' you are also 'being saved.' The glory you will see one day is not yet visible.

Therefore, hold on tightly to the hope that is in you. Your hope is based on God's promises. It is more secure than anything you can see with your eyes. Your struggles in this life, even though they are very real, do not negate the hope that is in you.

As you await your bodily redemption, serve God faithfully. Do not put your hope in things of this world. Remember those who have not been redeemed and lack this hope. Reach out to them with the gospel. Do not wait.

Psalm 147:7-11; 2 Corinthians 4:16-18

For what is our hope or joy or crown of boasting
before our Lord Jesus at his coming? Is it not you?
– 1 Thessalonians 2:19

One day, you will stand in front of Jesus. One confirmation that you have been faithful in your calling is converts—people you have led to Christ. People who have come to know the Lord because of you will be evidence of your faithfulness. They will be like your victory wreath.

Being able to point to people who have heard and followed Jesus because of you does not mean you will pridefully stand before God for what you have done. Rather, any boasting you do will be as thanks to God for the work He has done through you. Be faithful in fulfilling the roles God gives you. Influence other souls during the course of your life. Have Jesus on your lips, not just in your heart. Make disciples.

1 Chronicles 16:23-27; Romans 15:14-21

'Who can stand?'
– Revelation 6:17

Only people who believe in Jesus will stand. Everyone else who has rejected God's offer of forgiveness through His Son will fall. This reality should prompt you to examine yourself, as well as proclaim the hope and good news of Jesus Christ with others. He alone is able to save people from the great day of wrath that is coming.

How terrifying it will be to fall into God's hands apart from Christ! There is no annihilation or second chance for restoration. A person has one opportunity to accept Christ and stand up, and that is in each person's own lifetime. May God, in His mercy, grant you the opportunity to proclaim the good news, warning others in such a way that their hearts are open and receptive to embrace the gospel. Grace is still available. God is still waiting, but time is short. Everlasting peace comes only in Christ.

Nahum 1:5-6; Ephesians 6:13

'Did not our hearts burn within us while he
talked to us on the road,
while he opened to us the Scriptures?'
– Luke 24:32

Recall the first time you experienced the written words (Scripture) and the living Word (Jesus) simultaneously. Doubts were dispelled. Hope was confirmed. Your excitement escalated. You saw things in Scripture you had never seen before. What was unclear became clear. What was out of focus became in focus. What was invisible became visible.

Never forget that moment. Keep alive the memory of God's gracious acts toward you. Concentrate on knowing Jesus more. Prepare yourself for the future—and be ready to give a reason to others for the hope that is in you.

Jeremiah 23:29; John 6:63

December 6

'Is this not the reason you are wrong,
because you know neither the Scriptures
nor the power of God?'
– Mark 12:24

You may pride yourself on knowing what the Bible teaches. You may think you are able to show someone their error(s) pertaining to it quickly. In asking this inspired question, Jesus essentially says, 'Forget the answer—your assumptions on which the question is based are wrong. Let's start there.'

His meaning is that your thinking is wrong. You know very little about the things you speak about, such as angels, the afterlife, and the resurrection. Though they are beyond human understanding, let your descriptions of spiritual things come from God's Word and not from your own imagination. The Creator of the universe, for instance, is far greater than any human conception or depiction of Him. So don't reduce Him and His greatness to a human-made image or idea of who He is. Take God's Word seriously. Improve your intake of His Word. Study and meditate upon the Scriptures and God's mighty power.

Psalm 119:18; 2 Timothy 2:15

'What does this babbler wish to say?'

— Acts 17:18

You have probably been called a few names; some are far from polite. You are not alone. People laughed at Noah building the ark. Jehu's friends called the prophet—who Elisha sent to anoint Jehu king—a madman. Job's wife told him to curse God and die. A foolish nation told Micah to stop preaching. Festus said Paul was out of his mind. The religious rulers said Jesus was demon-possessed.

People of this world may disagree on many issues, but they are united in their condescension toward Christians. They are misguided and ignorant of God's grace. Even the thought that you personally know God and can proclaim what He says is ridiculous to them.

Scripture describes the cross as foolishness to those who are perishing. Yet you still need to proclaim the gospel. Engage the world's culture with respect. Look for opportunities to serve this dying world's people. Perhaps God will grant them repentance and they will come to their senses.

2 Chronicles 36:15-16; Mark 3:21

'Have you understood all these things?'
— Matthew 13:51

Sometimes, you need to step away from what you think you know so that you can see and enjoy the truth. Knowing something and understanding it are two different things. Jesus criticizes His followers for not understanding His words and only skimming the surface of what He is saying and doing. He has already told them that He has given them the mysteries of the kingdom, but they only gradually understand them.

Jesus could ask you the same inspired question. If your understanding of God's Word is truly growing, then you will be producing fruit. It is imperative that you put kingdom truths into practice and not just swim on the surface of what Jesus is teaching.

The mysteries of the kingdom are not something you just pick up by accident. Give concerted effort and concentrated attention to these truths. Seek to more profoundly experience and understand God's word. Delve deeply into the 'wellspring of life.' Doing so is a decision that is even more urgent if you do understand all these things.

Proverbs 4:5-9; 1 Thessalonians 2:13

'Who are you?'

– John 1:19

The emphasis is on 'you' in this inspired question. It is as if they are demanding to know, 'You—who do you think you are?' Of course, the 'you' is not you in this question. Neither is it Jesus, of whom people would go on to ask the same question. It is John the Baptist. His sole mission was to give testimony to Jesus. He wanted people to see Jesus clearly, even to the point of forsaking any personal prestige.

What a remarkable example for you to follow. People are looking for answers. Perhaps you are someone they turn to because you are in the public eye, have a large following, or are in a position of influence. Maybe you are not. Whatever your sphere of influence, you—like all Christians—are called to have the same attitude as John the Baptist. Understand that life is not about you. Don't just talk about yourself. Don't just focus on your story. You—like John—are only a voice in comparison to Christ. This type of humility will make you praiseworthy in God's eyes, and He will use you greatly because of it.

Deuteronomy 18:15-19; Acts 3:17-26

> *But if anyone has the world's goods and sees his*
> *brother in need, yet closes his heart against him,*
> *how does God's love abide in him?*
> — 1 John 3:17

This inspired question is not asking you if you will lay down your life for a fellow believer. It is not asking you if you will sell all your possessions and give the proceeds to the poor. It is asking you to do something easier and far less sacrificial. In light of what Jesus has done for you, your heart should be wide open to help other believers who are in material need. In fact, you cannot say that the love of God is in you if you refuse to help others when able.

Love for God and love for fellow Christians go hand-in-hand. There is no separating the two. This type of love is both generous and practical. You cannot merely speak of love; you must practice it. Part of practicing it is using your own resources to meet needs. Christian love indicates Christian faith. God wants His love to channel through you. You probably will not face martyrdom. But you will face (perhaps frequently) a fellow believer who has material needs you can meet. Be prompt to meet those needs.

Proverbs 3:27-28; 2 Corinthians 8:1-15

'What do you think about the Christ? Whose son is he?'
– Matthew 22:42

It is now your turn. Jesus wants you to answer a very specific theological question. The quick and traditional answer to this inspired question is, 'He is the Son of David,' which is the answer the Pharisees gave. Yet if you meditate on the passage, you will realize that King David in the Old Testament, whom Jesus quotes, would not have dared to have called himself or his son 'Lord.' Such an address would not have made sense. Thus, He is referring to the coming Messiah, whom he calls 'Lord.' Jesus, then, the Messiah, is far greater than merely being a descendant of David. He is Lord. He is seated at the right hand of God the Father.

Keep this teaching in the forefront of your mind and the center of your life. Reflect on Jesus in meditation. Don't unintentionally find yourself fighting against His will. Willingly volunteer to serve Him. Give yourself to Him. He is Lord.

2 Samuel 7:11-16; Romans 1:3-4

Why do you pass judgment on your brother?
Or you, why do you despise your brother?
– Romans 14:10

Do not cast doubt on someone else's salvation or status as a member of the body of Christ. Not only do you have no right, but you also endanger yourself. By sinfully criticizing others, you provoke God's judgment. You—like them—will ultimately answer to God.

So beware of your biases. Don't set yourself up to be hypocritical, unfriendly, or both. Avoid hasty judgments. Live with others according to God's Word. Bear with one another's failings. Live in harmony with each other. Let there be no divisions in the church. Rather, be of one mind, united in thought and purpose. Build up God's people. Let all you do be done in love.

Psalm 7:11; 2 Corinthians 5:10

DECEMBER 13

'Who is this, who even forgives sins?'
– Luke 7:49

Only God can forgive sins. Yet Jesus declares forgiveness here—and people witnessing His words are astonished. This is not something a mere prophet does. By forgiving sins, Jesus makes it impossible for you to be neutral about Him. You either question His authority or accept it. When you trust Him, He forgives you, He sets you free from sin, and He gifts you with peace with God.

Do not forget the joy of your salvation. Remember how sweet it was the first time you approached Jesus and realized you were in the divine presence of the very Son of God. Consider how you can take this truth and begin quieting your soul today. Rest in Him.

Psalm 51:4; Acts 10:42-43

What then is my reward?
– 1 Corinthians 9:18

By giving up certain things in this life, you may wonder what is in it for you. Sure, you are already blessed in the heavenly places. Your eternal reward makes angels watchful. But what about in your current life? Part of your reward includes contentment. Nothing in this world will keep your heart content, but grace will. If the eyes of your heart are not fixed on things in this world, then even the most challenging troubles you face will be minimal in comparison to what they would have been without the hope promised by God. Other changes and challenges will not be as troublesome either.

Oh, what freedom there is if you desire nothing on earth more than God! Consider these encumbrances. Die to the things of this world—evils such as the lust of the flesh, the lust of the eyes, and the pride of life. Live your life in such a way that you will be filled with joy when you look back on your life.

Psalm 37:3-9; Philippians 4:11-13

'Have you never read in the Scriptures:
"The stone that the builders rejected has become the
cornerstone;
this was the Lord's doing, and it is marvelous in our eyes"?'
– Matthew 21:42

Even if you are a lifelong student of the Scriptures, you could be unknowingly misinterpreting them or overlooking key passages.

You do not have a relationship with God the Father unless your foundation is God the Son. If you abide in the teaching of Christ, you have both the Father and the Son. Jesus is the Cornerstone of your faith and salvation, as the Old Testament prophesies. This is marvelous news—because it reveals and confirms God's grace. He continues to reach out to humanity. People the world once rejected will triumph. Jesus' death and resurrection have vindicated His coming to earth as the Son of God—and He now sits at the right hand of God.

Thank God for the gospel. Cast yourself upon His love, and love Him by keeping His commandments. Be diligent in reading and obeying the Scriptures. Set your heart on the things above. Seek and declare the whole counsel of God as spelled out in the Scriptures.

Psalm 118:22-23; Romans 9:30-33

'To what shall I compare the kingdom of God?'
– Luke 13:20

The kingdom of God may remain largely unseen, but its power is universal. Like yeast, it will permeate everything. It includes people from all over the world.

Look with the eyes of your heart for manifestations of God's kingdom and prepare to be amazed, surprised, and blessed. Look at your life again in this way. Be filled with a new hope, a new strength, and a new power as you wait for the new heaven, the new earth, and New Jerusalem to come down out of heaven from God. Stop looking at what you have not done or the things you have missed over the years—and realize that in God's kingdom, His grace is sufficient. What matters is faith working through love.

Whatever your circumstances are right now, they are only temporary. They are momentary. They can never rob you of the joy and glory that ultimately awaits you in God's kingdom. Bind yourself to this truth, and bind His Law to your mind. Submit yourself to it. Nothing can compare with the kindness of His grace or the holiness of His Law.

Daniel 2:44; Romans 14:17

'What are you seeking?'

— John 1:38

You heard a message about Jesus. Now you are following Him. You know He is guiding you. He is the Teacher. You are the disciple. But you still wonder what that relationship means and where exactly He is leading you. Incidentally, this inspired question comprises the first words of Jesus in John's gospel and clues you into several aspects of discipleship. Jesus sees those who follow Him and immediately beckons them onward.

What a great start to the life-changing moment of following Jesus and having a relationship with Him! Recall often your conversion experience. Remember the joy of your salvation. Don't forget your first love. He is your Teacher. Look entirely to Jesus, and stay teachable. You will never be happy if you do not. But you can always find reason for hope (and the happiness and joy that can come from that confidence, even in trials) if you do.

Psalm 51:12; Revelation 2:4

DECEMBER 18

'Do you believe in the Son of Man?'

— John 9:35

There is no telling how many people have experienced a divine healing yet cannot answer 'yes' to this inspired question. In fact, Jesus asks this question to a blind man He has just healed without yet identifying Himself, as if he was just a passerby, someone the man would not have even recognized. Now, face-to-face with his Healer—the Lord Jesus—he has the opportunity to answer this question. As a Jew who would have heard about the coming Messiah, he shows himself ready to believe in and follow the Son of Man—Jesus. Once Jesus tells him, 'the one speaking with you is He,' the man verbalizes his faith in Jesus and worships Him on the spot.

Having done the same, maintain this attitude and confession. Thank Him for any spiritual insight He might impart. Find time to worship Him every day. Sing hymns and new songs to God. Remember whose Presence is in your presence. Don't forget the joy of your salvation. In Him is everything pertaining to eternal life.

Psalm 2:10-12; Acts 7:56

'Why are you troubled, and why do doubts
arise in your hearts?'
– Luke 24:38

What a question! It encourages you to remember Who is present in your life and what that means. Troubles, doubts, and moods may swing back and forth, but Jesus is risen. When you don't abide in this truth, doubts will arise in your heart.

Don't just be persuaded about some impersonal facts about Jesus; remember that He is in your midst. Hear again His glorious words: 'Behold, I am with you always.' What a marvelous promise you have! Enter into the joy of the Lord. Conquer your doubts by looking steadily at Him. Live the Christian life in all its fullness because of this truth. Rest upon Jesus and His perfect work. Be diligent to enter that rest.

Jeremiah 4:14; Acts 8:22

DECEMBER 20

'For who has known the mind of the Lord,
or who has been his counselor?
Or who has given a gift to him that he might be repaid?'
– Romans 11:34-35

You already know the answer to each one of these inspired questions: 'No one!' God alone sits on high. He owes you nothing. He is all-sovereign, all-knowing, and completely free from obligation. Thankfully, in Christ you can grasp God's plan for salvation, experience the depth of His riches and wisdom and knowledge, and receive the gift He has freely given to you: the priceless gift of His Son, Jesus Christ.

Notice that there are many things you can know and know clearly, but that there are many more things that you cannot comprehend—not yet. Do not allow what you cannot understand to distract you from what you can. Place and keep your feet on the path to God. Surrender your will to His.

Isaiah 40:12-14; 1 Thessalonians 3:9

'Then why do the scribes say that first Elijah must come?'
– Matthew 17:10

You have heard questions like this. Someone refers to something a religious figure says, and then they ask you to confirm or deny it. Maybe they are trying to belittle or confuse someone. Maybe they lack confidence in Jesus' teaching. Perhaps they just want to interpret the Scriptures accurately. Regardless of the reason(s), confusion can overtake people as they try to understand the large amount of data and interpretations out there today.

Be diligent in prayer and in searching the Scriptures. God's Word must be our ultimate authority. (In the case of the scribes, they correctly determined that Elijah must come first. Yet they missed his coming.) Engage one another in reading God's Word. Cultivate the discipline of meditating on Scriptures. You will find yourself becoming more confident and less confused about questions such as the one above.

Malachi 4:5-6; Luke 1:8-17

'And we, what shall we do?'

– Luke 3:14

Once someone asks a question that affects everyone, it becomes contagious. Everyone wants to know the answer and to figure out how it applies to them. Abuse of authority is the issue here, such as whether it regards money or law enforcement—which are the two professions dealt with in the context of this inspired question.

The basic point is that you must be compassionate, loving, and just to everyone and not take advantage of them for your own personal gain. Be content with what you have. Look to meet the needs of those around you, including those who are less fortunate than yourself.

You probably do not have to leave your profession to go about your profession in a better way. But do seek every appropriate means of correcting your understanding and the way you work, so that you may be saved from error. Exercise authority from loving motives in a loving manner for loving purposes, just like Jesus. See everyone from a spiritual perspective.

Leviticus 25:43; Acts 22:10

'Who are you, Lord?'

— Acts 9:5

You may have acted out of ignorance or thought wrong things about Jesus and His followers. Now, you must admit your guilt. Begin walking by faith in Jesus—begin faithfully obeying His loving commands. Jesus is the Messiah. The good news about Him is true. You are one of His chosen children—a member of a royal priesthood.

Call out to Him. Humble yourself, and you will be exalted. Immerse yourself in the things of God.

1 Samuel 3; Matthew 8:27

'Who are you?
We need to give an answer to those who sent us.
What do you say about yourself?'

— John 1:22

There are times when someone might send another person to find out an answer from you or hear your self-description. It is certainly easier for the sender that way. Getting an answer through someone else's description of an event helps the sender avoid being personally confronted by the information. It also gives the sender time to digest what happened before making another move.

As you walk the walk today, strive to have the same type of attitude, response, and humility that John the Baptist had when he knew his words of warning would sometimes fall on deaf ears. He told the questioners (priests and Levites sent from Jerusalem) that he was someone who followed the Scriptures. He did what God commanded—and thus, he fulfilled the calling and purpose God had for his life. He wanted everyone to know about someone greater and more glorious than him: The Messiah, Jesus Christ.

Now go and do likewise. Honor God and not yourself with your dress, speech, and conduct. Inspire, challenge, and assure others of the worthwhile calling of Jesus. Hold on to God's Word. Speak truth.

Isaiah 40:3; Matthew 11:11-15

'Do you think that I have come to give peace on earth?'
— Luke 12:51

Everyone desires peace on earth. Peace characterizes God's forever rule. The prophet Isaiah calls Jesus the Prince of Peace. Yet Jesus' answer to His own question here is that His first coming was not peace and happiness for all. From His birth onward, Jesus' message of peace brought and continues to bring strife and division. People take opposing sides regarding Him. Different allegiances are professed. Opposite commitments are made. His coming—His birth—did not remove external trouble from this world. But it did increase hostility in the lives of those who follow Him as believers.

Having peace with God necessarily means having hostility with the world. By entering into a new relationship with God, you lose your life to this world. When this happens, something radical takes place. You see everything in a new light. You think differently. You feel differently. You act differently.

Some in your family may not like the new you. Your friends may not like the new you, either. You may call this hostility the dark side of Christmas, and it ought to remind you what is at the heart of discipleship: soberly counting the cost of placing Christ above everything and everyone else in your life ahead of all earthly attachments. Spend time today asking yourself, 'Who do I really love this Christmas season, and why?'

Hosea 14:9; Luke 2:34-35

'Are these things so?'
— Acts 7:1

When someone wrongly accuses you of something, use it as an opportunity to respond in love with your testimony and true Christian beliefs. People may think that they know the truth or think that they have correct doctrine, but you may recognize that they do not. God has now opened a door for you to lead them down the right path. They might even expect you to deny your faith or to accept their claims. But instead, reaffirm your Christian beliefs and proclaim your commitment to Christ.

Trust that God will work through you. Be strong and bear His light.

1 Chronicles 16:8-36; Luke 21:10-19

DECEMBER 27

'Lord, what about this man?'
– John 21:21

You are not alone in comparing yourself to other people. Even the apostle Peter did it here. Nevertheless, that does not make it right, commendable, or wise. In fact, Jesus puts Peter in his place and makes it clear that he has no business comparing himself to anyone else.

Similarly, God has given you specific commands to follow. You need to examine yourself and live accordingly. God will judge you based on what you do or do not do, and not in comparison to anyone else. Therefore, do not deceive yourself by comparing your life and good works with anyone else's. Submit to God's will for your life alone—and focus on Him.

Exodus 20:17; 2 Corinthians 10:12

DECEMBER 28

'O Sovereign Lord, holy and true, how long before you will judge and avenge our blood on those who dwell on the earth?'
– Revelation 6:10

We live in a hard, broken, and hostile world that awaits Judgment Day. It's a world where people kill Christians without immediate consequences. This powerful, inspired question comes from Christian martyrs who have died faithfully and gone to heaven. They are not crying out for personal revenge. Rather, they want to know when justice will be done. God's reputation is on the line. He will be considered an unjust judge if He does not punish sin. He has promised that vengeance is His—and that He will repay. He must demonstrate His holiness and standard of truth by bringing sinners to justice.

This is certainly not the first time this type of question occurs in the Bible. It is actually a well-worn question. Although you will not know the timing, you can be certain that God will vindicate the blood of the martyrs and execute perfect justice. In the meantime, martyrs will continue to enjoy their rightful place in heaven.

People who harm God's children should be frightened. They will not get away with it forever. In Christ, then, bear whatever comes your way.

Psalm 13; Luke 18:1-8

For what son is there whom his father does not discipline?
— Hebrews 12:7

Your Father in heaven loves you. He is committed to you. He wants you to be victorious. Therefore, He mercifully disciplines you. He disciplines you as His child because you are His child.

Rejoice in this. Proper discipline is an essential part of good family life. One of the primary parental responsibilities is appropriate discipline, and parents neither spoil nor ignore their children. Gratefully accept God's discipline. Humble yourself under His mighty hand so that He will lift you up. Keep His commandments so that you may prosper in all that you do and wherever you go. Dwell in repentance.

Proverbs 13:24; 2 Corinthians 12:7-10

Now who is there to harm you if you are
zealous for what is good?
— 1 Peter 3:13

Unbelievers persecute Christians every day. The inspired question here, however, asks how often someone harms you for doing good things. That would be uncommon. Usually, you receive your reward when you do what is good. Of course, harm to you can and does still happen. The best example of such harm being done to an innocent person is Christ. He suffered a criminal's death on a cross, but never sinned.

You, too, might be wrongly accused, judged, or condemned. Therefore, you need to know that God will bless you if you suffer for doing right. Life's greatest tragedies cannot destroy your ultimate hope. Your confidence in God will be fully rewarded. Though your hopes in this life may be utterly dashed into pieces, God's promises for the future always remain unbreakable.

The Christian life includes being courageous, having zeal, displaying boldness, and modeling ourselves after Jesus. We know He was resurrected, so we can understand the blessing in suffering. Blessed are you when you occupy your time with being zealous for what is good.

Isaiah 41:8-13; Revelation 2:10

Why do you marvel?

– Revelation 17:7

People often express amazement for things or people that are not really amazing. They may say how impressed they are and they may marvel at what should shock or appall them. But the problem is this: They are not focusing on God—the only One worthy of our reverence and wonder. God is the only One whose kingdom is an everlasting kingdom, and whose dominion endures from generation to generation.

Truth be told, we all marvel—or don't marvel—at things or people because we don't see them for what or who they really are. We judge partially because we only know partially. We cannot see someone's heart. We cannot know someone's nature. We don't have a window to look into anyone's soul.

What a great question for you to frequently remember to ask: 'Why do you marvel?'

Daniel 4:16; Acts 8:9-11

Christian Focus Publications

Our mission statement —

STAYING FAITHFUL

In dependence upon God we seek to impact the world through literature faithful to His infallible Word, the Bible. Our aim is to ensure that the Lord Jesus Christ is presented as the only hope to obtain forgiveness of sin, live a useful life and look forward to heaven with Him.

Our books are published in four imprints:

CHRISTIAN
FOCUS

Popular works including biographies, commentaries, basic doctrine and Christian living.

CHRISTIAN
HERITAGE

Books representing some of the best material from the rich heritage of the church.

MENTOR

CF4•K

Books written at a level suitable for Bible College and seminary students, pastors, and other serious readers. The imprint includes commentaries, doctrinal studies, examination of current issues and church history.

Children's books for quality Bible teaching and for all age groups: Sunday school curriculum, puzzle and activity books; personal and family devotional titles, biographies and inspirational stories — because you are never too young to know Jesus!

Christian Focus Publications Ltd,
Geanies House, Fearn, Ross-shire,
IV20 1TW, Scotland, United Kingdom.
www.christianfocus.com